Complete
Bike
Maintenance

MBI Publishing Company

Contents

Written and edited by: Fred Milson

Studio photography: Steve Behr

Tim Ridley

Polly Wreford

Illustrations: Ian Bott

Page make-up: Jeremy Phillips

Production manager: Kevin Perrett

Fred Milson has asserted his right to be identified as the author of this work.

First published 1995
This edition published 1999
Reprinted 2000 (with minor amendments)
Reprinted 2002
First published in 2002 by
MBI Publishing Company, 380 Jackson Street, Suite 200,
St. Paul, MN 55101-3885 USA

Library of Congress Cataloging-in-Publication Data Available
ISBN 0-76033-1330-X

Printed in Hong Kong

CHAPTER 1

KNOW YOUR BIKE

This book has been written using just a few technical words and as little cycling jargon as possible. But you will find it useful to pick up a few essential words right at the start.

Name that part

OTHER STYLES OF SADDLE

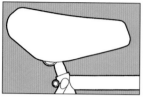

WOMEN'S SADDLE
*Specially designed saddle, can
be fitted to almost any bike.*

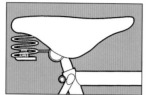

MATTRESS SADDLE
For utility bikes only.

SADDLE

SEAT POST

REAR BRAKE

WHEEL NUTS

MULTIPLE FREEWHEEL
OR CASSETTE

CABLE STOP

SEAT TUBE

FRONT
DERAILLEUR

PEDAL

ALTERNATIVE
GEARING SYSTEMS

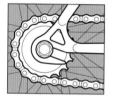

**SINGLE-SPEED
FREEWHEEL**
*Mainly used on kids'
bikes.*

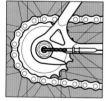

HUB GEARS,
*As used on most
utility bikes.*

GEAR CABLE

REAR DERAILLEUR

CHAIN STAYS

CHAIN

BOTTOM
BRACKET

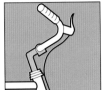

ALTERNATIVE HANDLEBARS

DROP HANDLEBARS
For racing, sports, and touring bikes.

FLATS
For hybrids and utilities.

RAISED BARS
Used on utility bikes and MTBs.

BAR ENDS

HANDLEBARS

STEM

BRAKE LEVER

HEADSET

HEAD TUBE

TOP TUBE

FRONT BRAKE

DOWN TUBE

FRONT WHEEL

SPOKE

TIRE

CRANKS

FORKS

RIM

HUB

CHAINRINGS

VARIOUS TYPES OF TIRES

KNOBBY TIRES
For off-road mountain bikes.

MOUNTAIN BIKE SLICKS
For use on the road.

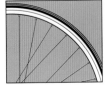

700 C x 27 INCH
Tires for racers and hybrids.

QUICK RELEASE

TIRE VALVE

Adult bikes

Mountain bikes outsell every other type of bike 10 to 1 because they are fun, fashionable and fit for use in town and country. But even if you already have a bike, you should still take a look at other types that might suit your style of cycling better.

Although there are at least 100 million bikes in the United States, another 20 million or so are sold every year. Most of these are Mountain Bikes (MTBs), but slowly, hybrids are gaining ground. Hybrid bikes are a cross between an MTB and a road bike, combining the strength of a mountain bike with the easy pedaling of a road machine. They're a very good compromise for riders who mostly cycle in town and on normal roads, but do not want a racer.

Thoroughbred racers also sell, but only in small numbers. However, like top mountain bikes, they are now built using manufacturing techniques and materials developed in the aerospace industry and offer incredible value for money. Sales of racers are on the increase in the U.S., especially after the success of Lance Armstrong in the Tour de France.

See chapter 10, which goes into frame design in more detail.

MOUNTAIN BIKES
The key to mountain bike (MTB) popularity is their versatility. The small frames and 26in wheels with well-cushioned tires originated in California among riders who enjoyed plummeting down mountain sides. By coincidence, the same features suit city riders who need to bump up and down curbs and ride through potholes. The bike shown below is one variation on the Y-frame design. These are now very popular in the mid-price range; they are very strong and are nearly always fitted with suspension. But normal MTB frames with round tubes and preferably a sloping top tube are unbeatable as long as value for money is concerned.

RACING BIKE

Welded aluminum frames are now standard for racing bikes. On the road, racers are much faster than MTBs but not so comfortable, although aluminum frames and new types of gel saddles will take the worst out of the bumps. Touring and Cyclo-cross bikes are closely related to racers but have stronger wheels and a wider range of gears.

WOMAN'S BIKE

An open frame MTB bike allows you the option of riding in a skirt, but a mountain bike with a sloping top tube is the better option for most women.

UTILITY BIKE

Best for city use over short distances, the upright riding position means you can wear fairly formal clothes and still cycle to work. New types of hub and derailleur gears, specially designed to lighten the load on utility riders, are now in production.

HYBRID BIKE

Hybrids have a modified MTB frame, usually with a sloping top tube. Not only does this keep the frame light and agile at low speeds, it also gives a lot more clearance over the top tube when you are waiting at traffic lights or jumping curbs. Look for brazed-on carrier fittings, a wide range of gears, and light but robust wheels and tires when you are buying. Suspension forks are now available on some models as well as a spring seat post or shock post to absorb bumps.

Men's bike set up

A good riding position doesn't just make you comfortable, it helps you to ride more efficiently. It mainly depends on sharing your weight evenly around the bike.

When you take over a bike, set the basic riding position using the advice on the opposite page. Then ride around for a few days while you get used to it. Your new bike may feel strange at first, but if the riding position is right, you will feel that your weight is being shared fairly evenly between the saddle and the handlebars.

In addition, you must find a comfortable position for the hands, without feeling stretched out. This is particularly important if you are riding a sports bike or a racer. When looking at these, remember that you are not expected to use the 'drops' all the time. There are alternative hand positions on the brake levers and the top part of the handlebars, which should allow a comfortable back angle of 30° to 40°. Do not forget that if need be, you can install a longer or shorter handlebar stem.

If you're not comfortable on the saddle, check first that it is horizontal. If it is, try moving it half an inch forward, then an inch back. There is no ideal position–you have to find out what suits you. Some riders feel better with the saddle nose pointed up just a fraction, but don't go any further than that. Try a different saddle if you really can't get comfortable.

When buying a new bike or frame, go for the smallest one that fits you. As a guide, most of the seat post should be out of the frame when the saddle height is correct. If you buy a frame that is too big, the basic proportions of the frame will be wrong.

UTILITY BIKES
Frames on utility bikes are normally laid well back, so most of your weight naturally falls on the saddle. There is no way of avoiding this completely, but you could try lowering the handlebars or installing straight ones if you're really uncomfortable. Toe clips aren't usually fitted to utilities, but you should still try to keep the ball of your foot over the pedal axle so that you can pedal efficiently. Because utility bikes are mostly used for short journeys around town, the saddle can be set lower than normal. This allows the rider to plant one foot flat on the ground while sitting in the saddle, which is more comfortable when waiting at traffic lights and other hold ups.

Frame size

MOUNTAIN BIKES
Mountain bike frames come in several different styles and so riders tend to go for a greater variety of riding positions than they do on other bikes. Set the basic saddle position in the same way as a racer, but you may feel happier with slightly more bend in the leg. In addition, the back should be at roughly 45° to the ground so that you can see ahead without having to crank your head backwards. A 45° angle also throws your weight on to the handlebars. This holds the front wheel down and helps you to keep control of the steering at speed.You may have install a different stem or handlebars to achieve this.

1 Frame size is usually measured from the center of the bottom bracket axle to the center of the top tube. However, changes in frame design are making this system less useful. Try to get a test ride before deciding which size you need.

2 Frames for racers, touring bikes, and men's utility bikes are all roughly the same height from floor to top tube. You should aim for at least an inch and a half of clearance between the top tube and your crotch when your feet are planted flat on the floor.

3 Mountain bike frames have a different shape, partly to ensure you have at least three inches clearance over a horizontal top tube. But most MTBs have a sloping top tube, and with this shape of frame, top tube clearance should be at least 4 or 5 in.

Sports bikes and racers

1 Set the basic saddle height first, wearing the shoes you will usually ride in. After a few days, you will probably find you can ride faster with the saddle a little higher so that your leg is only very slightly bent when the pedal is at its lowest point.

2 One way to set the saddle position is to hang a plumb line from the knee, with the cranks horizontal. Then adjust the saddle until the plumb line passes through the pedal axle. However, it's usually better to experiment for yourself.

BASIC SADDLE HEIGHT
Whatever type of bike you ride, set the saddle height so that when sitting on the bicycle with your leg fully stretched, you can place the ball of your foot onto the ground quite comfortably. That means your leg will be bent a little when the pedal is at its lowest point. This is only the starting point, so try a few

rides before deciding whether moving the saddle up or down a little would suit you better. Don't worry if it feels as if your leg muscles are being stretched, the stiffness should soon go away. If you still feel uncomfortable after a few days, see page 13 for tips on improving your riding position.

Women's bike set up

Most women are distinctly uncomfortable on most bikes. That is because the frame and the components are designed for the male, not the female body. Luckily, some simple adjustments can make the majority of women riders comfortable.

Women's bikes with open frames are still around in large numbers and you can still buy them, even MTB–style frames. On the other hand, this type of frame is not stiff or strong enough for anything more than short city runs. Far better, even if you want the option of cycling in a skirt, is an MTB or hybrid bike with a steeply sloping top tube.

However, choosing a sound frame design is only the start. Most riders, male and female, ride a bike with a frame that's too large. Men can usually get away with this because the proportions are basically right. On the other hand, the legs of an average woman are proportionally longer, but the body is proportionally shorter, the hands are smaller and the pelvis is a different shape.

So the first step is to choose a bike with the smallest frame you can. Women of average height will be fine with a 15in (38cm) MTB frame or a 19in (49cm) racing or touring frame, although taller women may have to go up to a 17in (43cm) MTB or a 21in (54cm) racer.

The next check is to see if you can use the brake levers comfortably. If not, it may be possible to adjust the reach, as shown on the next page. If this does not work, it may be possible to install smaller levers or special handlebars.

As for saddle height, this should be set the same as a man's bike. If the small frame does not allow you to raise the saddle enough, it is very easy to install a longer seat post. Some women will also need short 165mm (6.5in) cranks. Similarly, if the handlebars are too much of a stretch, it is pretty straightforward to install a stem that brings them closer. Incidentally, most women prefer the handlebars to be just a little below saddle height, not well below it as men do. This is sometimes a matter of adjusting the height of the stem, but in other cases, you may have to install a stem with a higher lift.

Finally, perhaps most important of all is the saddle. Saddles for women are wider at the back, shorter overall, and have more padding. There are many different designs on the market, so try a selection before deciding which is the one for you.

This is a well equipped MTB-style woman's bike sold mainly for use in the city. The fenders, pannier carrier, and built-in lighting also make it suitable for gentle touring, say 30 or 40 miles a day. The large diameter down tubes help to compensate for the reduced rigidity of the open frame design but the handling, when fully loaded, inevitably suffers compared with the similar bike below.

The full diamond frame version of this model is much more rigid and handles more securely. But more important, the sloping top tube gives nearly as much standover height, so it is still possible to wear a skirt occasionally, without sacrificing strength and handling qualities.

Adjusting the brake levers

1 Check to see if you can reach the brake levers without changing your grip on the handlebars. V brakes only need two fingers for full power, but the first joint should wrap comfortably around the lever.

2 If you can not wrap your fingers around the lever easily, look for an adjuster screw in the angle between the brake lever and the handlebar. You will need a Phillips screwdriver or a hexagon key for the job.

3 Then wind the adjuster in clockwise until you can apply the brakes comfortably. If there is no adjuster, or the adjuster does not make much difference, fit an alternative pair of brake levers.

Further modifications

1 To allow for proportionately longer legs, it is very simple to install an extra-long seat post on most frames. Seat post diameter does vary, so make sure you get the correct size. Do not pull it out further than the limit mark.

2 If your problem is discomfort over bumps, the answer is a shock post. This fits in place of an ordinary seat post and absorbs the bumps by means of a strong internal spring. It will fit a female-friendly saddle as well.

3 If you want to experiment with different riding positions, consider fitting an adjustable stem. Undoing the front bolt allows you to raise or lower the handlebars, which also alters the distance to the handlebars a little.

YOUR RIDING POSITION IS NOT RIGHT IF:

Your bottom is sore after a few miles.
Cure: Check that saddle is the correct height and exactly horizontal, then try a different saddle.

You continually slip towards the nose of the saddle.
Cure: Check the saddle angle.

You feel stretched out over the frame.
Cure: Shorter handlebar stem.

Your neck and shoulders get stiff or ache.
Cure: Raise the handlebars so you can look forwards without kinking your neck.

Your wrists hurt.
Cure: Raise the handlebars or lower the saddle.

Your knees hurt.
Cure: Check saddle height is correct. Make sure that pedals turn freely and that your feet are not held too firmly in the toe clips.

Your feet hurt.
Cure: Wear stiffer shoes, preferably proper cycling shoes. Do not pull your toe straps so tight.

HANDLEBAR STEMS

Women riders tend to lean too far forward and crouch over the saddle unless the bike is a good fit. If you notice this happening, consider fitting an angled stem. This will lift the handlebars without pushing you too far back for efficient pedaling. See page 142 for information on how to do this.

WOMEN'S BIKE SPECIALISTS

If you cannot get comfortable on a mass-produced bike but are determined to continue cycling, or you are unusually small, check out the specialist cycle builders and retailers who advertise in bike magazines. Among the various items they offer are made-to-measure bikes, usually based on ultra small frames installed with 26in (66cm) wheels and specially shortened cranks. Some specialists will even lend you a saddle for a few days so you can check it for comfort.

Kids' bikes

When kids learn to ride a bike, they gain so many things: self-confidence, early mechanical skills, road sense, even adventure. Provided they get good training in road skills right from the start, it's a very positive experience.

Size counts for a lot when it comes to children's bikes. The temptation is to buy a bike that a child will grow into, but you should resist. They will find it much more difficult to gain confidence on a bike they can only just control.

Tiny 14in wheel and 16in wheel bikes are usually fitted with a very crude drivetrain and steering bearings. Once you are looking at 20in wheel bikes, go for one with adult style steering bearings and drivetrain, especially if you are buying second-hand. That will make it easier to get hold of replacement parts and easier to do routine maintenance as well. However, multi-speed gears are unnecessary and are likely to be a constant source of problems until the child can handle a 24in bike.

24in WHEEL BIKES
From eleven years of age onwards, a scaled down adult bike is fine. If you go for one with a 14 or 15in (35 or 38cm) frame and a sloping top tube, there will be plenty of step-over clearance and it will allow for several years of growth. Don't forget that you can fit a longer seat post in the years to come but toe clips should only be fitted from twelve years of age onwards. If you plan to keep the bike for some time, it is worth going for a bike one or two steps up from budget level as the higher-quality components will need less maintenance and they will be much easier to work on.

20in WHEEL BIKES

Suitable for girls and boys eight to eleven years old, this size of bike can either have a single gear, which means simplicity, crash resistance, and low maintenance, or scaled-down adult equipment, including gearing. This is exciting but may not keep working for very long. The one shown has an immensely strong Y-frame, a design based on the latest adult MTBs.

PLAY BIKES WITH 14in WHEELS

Up to 4 years old. Good for giving the very youngest children a taste for cycling but do not leave the training wheels on for too long because they can become a substitute for learning to ride properly.

16in WHEEL BIKES

One stage up from play bikes, 16in wheel machines suit kids from $4^{1}/_{2}$ to $6^{1}/_{2}$ years old.

GIRL'S BIKE WITH 20in WHEELS

A classic girl's bike, with absolutely no frills. Now that the frame on most kids' bikes has a sloping top tube, it is hard to see much future for this type of machine.

Kids' bike set up

Don't leave your child's riding position to chance or other kids. Set it up carefully for safety and easy control.

Until a child has mastered adult level bike control and road awareness, insist on setting their riding position yourself and check it every few months as they grow. The main thing is to keep the saddle low enough to allow them to plant the balls of both feet firmly on the ground, while still sitting on the bike. When they get old enough to handle a 24in wheel bike, set the saddle height as you would on an adult bike.

There should be at least 2in of standover clearance above the top tube on a conventional frame and 3in on a sloping top tube frame. Less clearance than that means the frame is too large.

Don't forget to check the reach as well. If a child has to lean forward to reach the handlebars, maybe you should fit a stem with a shorter extension.

Whatever style of bike they ride, children should sit more upright than adults to encourage them to look ahead down the road.

Parents report that the easiest way to teach kids how to ride is to set the saddle height low enough to let them plant their feet on the ground with the bike upright and legs slightly bent, then remove the pedals as explained on page 84 and let the kid loose. They'll naturally start to scoot the bike along with their feet, learning how to steer and use the brakes as they go. Once they've gained some confidence, the saddle can be raised little by little until they're starting to lift both feet off the ground. At that point, introduce straight line and slalom exercises and once they can steer accurately, on with the pedals and away!

FEET FLAT ON THE GROUND

Until a child has close to well perfect bike control, keep the saddle low so that they can slip off it and get their feet down quickly if necessary. This will help to prevent scraped knees and damage to the bike. This bike has 20in wheels with reflectors fitted between the spokes to draw the motorist's attention both day and night.

STAY IN YOUR PLACE

When you are out with the children, insist they ride in front of you so that you can see everything that's happening. Do not ride too close or you'll have to keep on braking and there is also the danger of a crash if somebody in front stops unexpectedly.

SLOPING TOP TUBE

The sloping top tube design works well for younger children, giving plenty of standover height.

SPECIAL BITS

Most kids' bikes are small versions of an adult's bike. But some have special headsets and drivetrains that work in a very different way. The headsets are similar to the Aheadset featured on page 162, while the drivetrain and bottom bracket is covered on page 98.

TINY BIKES FOR TINY RIDERS

An enclosed space or garden is best for very young riders, where they can pick up self confidence in complete safety. Set up slalom tracks and figure-eight steering tests for fun and to develop and improve control skills.

BMX bikes

Riding a BMX develops fantastic bike control skills and opens up a world of excitement and friendly competition.

BMXs are designed for maximum bike control at slow speeds. The frames are built for strength rather than speed and the basic design does not vary a lot, although there are various styles of riding such as freestyle, stunt, and off-road. Only one size of frame is normally available, though the saddle adjusts up and down to cater for riders of varying height.

There is only one gear on these bikes, so you can only vary the gearing by fitting a larger or smaller chainring. However, basic BMXs use a one-piece drivetrain, see page 98, so you cannot change the gearing on these anyway. Higher up the range, the drivetrains are similar to a normal cotterless and it is possible to change the chainring, see page 90.

Maybe the hardest part of a BMX to understand is the braking system. Most BMXs are fitted with compact U brakes in front and back. However, many tricks involve spinning the handlebars, which would be impossible without a special device called a rotor head. This features a back brake cable that splits into two near the brake lever. The cable adjusters screw into a loose plate at the top of the headset with the nipples located in the middle plate. A second pair of cables connects to the middle and lower plates but join into one again before reaching the back brake. When you spin the handlebars, the stem and headset revolve but the cable mounting plates stay still.

Some BMX riding styles and practices place an extraordinary load on the frame and mechanical parts, so bear in mind that the guarantee probably only covers normal off-road riding.

SAFETY POINT

When any bike is on the road, including any BMX, the law says it must have two independent brakes, both of them in working order.

We strongly endorse this point and, bearing in mind that riding without brakes is a BMX street fashion, we urge parents to check from time to time that the brakes have not been removed from any BMX bikes in their household.

Setting up a BMX bike

1 The front U brake is fitted with a cable pipe that fits into a socket on one of the brake arms. Check occasionally that the cable pipe still moves freely. When setting up the brakes, keep the straddle wire as short as possible, for maximum braking efficiency.

2 When front or rear pegs are fitted, you'll have to use a socket set with a 10 or 12in extension to tighten up or undo the wheels nuts. This is not the easiest task, but if you get somebody else to steady the handlebars or the saddle, it will help a lot.

3 To check the chain tension, try lifting the chain at the mid-point of its bottom run. It is correct when you can lift it ½in. To adjust, undo the wheel nuts, move the wheel to the new position, check it is central, and tighten the wheel nuts a little at a time.

4 To prevent distortion of the clamp when adjusting the handlebar angle, undo one nut half a turn, then the diagonally opposite nut the same amount. Undo the other two in a similar way and continue half a turn at a time. Reverse procedure when tightening.

Adjusting rotor rear brakes

1 Screw in the cable adjuster on the frame as far as possible. Then loosen off the straddle wire yoke and move it up the cable until it is about ½in from the frame and retighten. This will help to reduce the amount of pull needed to apply the brakes.

2 Release one end of the straddle wire and run it around the yoke. Refit the straddle cable to the brake arm, tension the straddle wire with pliers, and then tighten the clamp bolt. There should be a right angle between the brake arm and the straddle cable.

3 Now check the cable assembly just below the handlebars. Make sure that the middle plates are free to move and lubricated lightly. Adjust the brake cables so that both moving plates are an equal distance apart at their ends and level with the ground.

4 Test the tension on the top section of the rear brake cables. If they're slack, increase the tension using the cable adjuster near the brake lever and the adjusters on the top plate. Then test the back brake, using the cable adjuster on the frame if necessary.

BMX PEDALS
If the frame or cage around the pedals gets bent or distorted, fit replacements immediately, or they can cause accident or injury.

As the pedals take a battering every time a BMX is dropped, and that can be quite often, fit good quality replacements as they will take the punishment much better.

Personal safety

Wearing a helmet is voluntary, not a legal requirement, but very few bike riders are now bold enough to venture on to the roads without one.

Don't rush in and buy a helmet in the first shop you come to. Find one that has a good selection of helmets from a wide variety of different makers and employs experienced staff. Then ask them to advise you about the suitability of the different designs for your kind of cycling.

Try on plenty of types and makes of helmet and don't give up until you find one with a really good fit. One test is that if you are able to move the helmet backwards and forwards with your hands when the chin strap is properly adjusted and fastened, it is too big. Not only will it be uncomfortable, it will also give you much less protection and may even slip off when it's put to the test.

Look particularly for well designed ways of adjusting the fit, such as interchangeable pads of varying thicknesses to install in pockets around the edge of the helmet. The other feature to look for is a nape strap or retention bracket at the back of the neck.

Apart from fit, the other factor governing comfort is ventilation. Make sure there are plenty of air channels running from front to back because although a helmet may not feel hot in the shop, it certainly will after ten miles of hard pedaling. However, too many ventilation channels can weaken a helmet fatally, so make sure there are plenty of strengthening elements running across the helmet as well.

When buying a helmet in the U.S. be sure that it meets the minimum standards of the U.S. Consumer Product Safety Commission.

1 Make sure you buy a well-fitting helmet. If the fit is right, the helmet will sit quite low on your brow, but high enough to allow unobstructed vision when you're looking upwards or sideways.

2 Inside the helmet, if a retention bracket is fitted, the micro-adjustable fastening system enables you to position the bracket accurately, just below the bulge of the skull.

1 You will need a waterproof jacket sooner or later. It will only be used in bad weather, so fluorescent yellow with strips of reflective material is the sensible option.

2 Proper cyclists gloves are a good investment. Go for ones with gel-padded palms. They reduce vibration from the road as well as protecting your hands in a crash.

3 Child's cycling gear is available in all sorts of designs. Encourage helmet use by buying a helmet that fits in with the child's heroes, or their favorite stories.

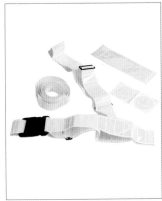

4 Perhaps the best values in bike safety are reflective belts and arm bands. They are effective night and day. But the most effective thing you can do is install reflectors on the pedals.

3 When properly adjusted, a retention bracket prevents the helmet from tipping backwards. If this happens, it is uncomfortable and reduces the effectiveness of the helmet.

4 The straps must fit naturally either side of the ears. If they don't, then choose another helmet. The adjusters should sit below the lobes and the buckle tuck under the chin.

5 Some helmets are fitted with an external adjuster to get the fit exactly right, but most manufacturers rely on interchangeable pads of varying thickness to do this.

AFTER A CRASH

The foam shock absorbing material in a helmet compresses during a crash and doesn't regenerate. As a result, some manufacturers offer to inspect a helmet after a crash. The foam also becomes less effective over a period of time, so it is best to replace any helmet that has been in an accident, however slight. To encourage this, some makes offer free replacement after an accident. However, bear in mind that if you leave the cheapest helmets aside, paying a higher price does not necessarily get you a better product.

KIDS' HELMETS

To be fully effective, helmets for children have to be relatively larger than adult ones, so they sometimes look as if they are perched on top of the head. However, they must fit at least as well as any adult helmet and according to the same guidelines.

CHAPTER 2

TOOLS & TECHNIQUES

Take a look at the tools you already have in the house and the garage—you have probably got most of the basic stuff you need already. Now for a few ideas on how to use them safely and effectively.

Basic tool kit

Most people spend more than half their bike maintenance time cleaning and oiling the chain and the gear mechanisms. If you spend less time than that, or no time at all, you are not doing it right.

Sooner or later you will need most of the tools shown on this page, although you are unlikely to need them all at once. You will certainly need a few bike-friendly lubricants before you can do even the most basic maintenance. A general purpose aerosol spray can be used for most jobs but the specialized bike lubricants are more effective and last much longer, especially in the wet. The ones that leave a solid lubricant behind when they evaporate are probably best. For chains, however, many riders use a specialist chain lubricant, perhaps backed up by an aerosol type. So even if the top layer of lube gets washed off in a downpour, the lower layer will remain active and prevent excessive wear.

METRIC WRENCHES
You will mainly use the 8, 9, 10 and 11mm sizes, both box and open-ended.

SCREWDRIVERS
Normal screwdrivers are used for adjusting gears. Phillips screwdrivers sizes 1 and 2 are also vital.

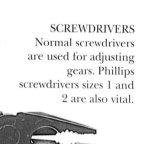

LARGE PLIERS
For pulling cables but never cutting them. Smaller types are sometimes useful too.

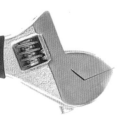

CRESCENT WRENCH
For use only on headsets and bottom brackets, although a specifically designed wrench is better.

SPECIALLY-FORMULATED WATERPROOF GREASE

CHAIN MAINTENANCE

DEGREASER

SPECIALIZED CHAIN LUBE

CHAIN CLEANING MACHINE

ENVIRONMENTALLY FRIENDLY DEGREASER

BRUSH FOR USE WITH SOLVENT

DRY CHAIN LUBE

OILS AND GREASES

HIGH QUALITY
LUBE FOR MTBs

TOOTHBRUSH
You will sometimes find
it easier and quicker to
degrease components
with a toothbrush than
anything else.

UTILITY KNIFE
For cutting handlebar
tape, electrical insulation,
and cable tidies.

GREASE INJECTOR PACK
FOR USE ON BEARINGS
AND BRAKE PIVOTS

COPPER-BASED
ANTI-SEIZE GREASE

HEX KEYS
The standard type is
shown here but the long
workshop type is much
more useful on bikes.
You will need sizes up to
8 or 10mm.

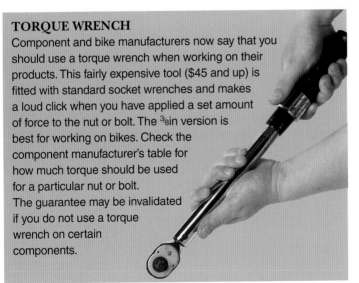

TORQUE WRENCH
Component and bike manufacturers now say that you
should use a torque wrench when working on their
products. This fairly expensive tool ($45 and up) is
fitted with standard socket wrenches and makes
a loud click when you have applied a set amount
of force to the nut or bolt. The $\frac{3}{8}$in version is
best for working on bikes. Check the
component manufacturer's table for
how much torque should be used
for a particular nut or bolt.
The guarantee may be invalidated
if you do not use a torque
wrench on certain
components.

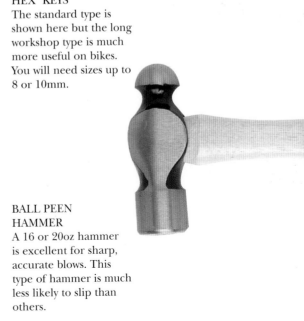

**BALL PEEN
HAMMER**
A 16 or 20oz hammer
is excellent for sharp,
accurate blows. This
type of hammer is much
less likely to slip than
others.

Working techniques

Once you have got hold of the tools, you have to learn how to use them without damaging the things you are working on.

Nuts and bolts have a six-sided shape which is usually spoken of as a hexagon. Damage the hexagon with a badly fitting wrench and it will be a nuisance until the day you replace it. To avoid this, use a tightly fitting box wrench whenever you can. If you have to use an open-ended wrench and it feels loose on the hexagon, try to find one with a better fit. If you can't, try wedging a small coin or a washer in the jaws of the wrench.

The length of each wrench is related to the amount of force needed to tighten each size of nut, so don't use a lot of force. You should be able to tighten up anything sufficiently using the pull of three fingers. If the amount of effort required to tighten a nut or bolt suddenly increases, stop immediately as something is probably about to break or you are pulling the thread out.

You can apply a bit of extra force when tightening a nut or bolt that keeps on coming loose but it's better to fit a self-locking nut or use Loctite.

Socket head fixings (otherwise known as Allen bolts) look great on bikes because they are so neat. But, unlike nuts or bolts, which you can nearly always remove one way or another, damaged socket head fixings can be almost impossible to remove. So check that the socket is clean to ensure that the hex key goes to the bottom of the socket and make sure also that the hex key is an exact fit. Don't use silver-painted hex keys as they are too soft and usually fit very badly. If you have a handful of mixed hex keys, only use the ones with a metric size engraved on the side. That should ensure they will be appropriate for bicycles.

Phillips screwdrivers are quite likely to damage the screw heads unless you use one with a hardened tip and apply plenty of force to the end of the handle to prevent it from slipping.

1 Whenever possible, use a box wrench or socket in preference to any other type of wrench. They grip a nut or bolt on all six corners, so if you are careful, there is little chance of the wrench slipping and damaging the bolt head.

2 An open-ended wrench is more likely to slip because it grips only two corners. When you've no choice but to use one, try to prevent it from slipping by steadying your hand against another component nearby.

5 Socket head fixings tend to fill with mud. So clean them out and check that the hex key goes all the way to the base of the socket before using any force. Otherwise the hex key may slip around in the socket and damage it.

6 When a socket head fixing is buried deep in a component, you will only be able to reach it with the long leg of a hex key. To increase the leverage, slip a close-fitting length of tubing over the shorter end. Do not use when tightening.

3 A set of open-ended wrenches will be very useful for holding a bolt while you loosen the nut. You will have to do this when a bolt turns before the nut comes undone and when undoing brake cable clamps.

4 Socket sets aren't usually regarded as bike tools but they are ideal for jobs where the nut is buried. On some pedals, for example, you can only reach the cone lock nut with a socket and extension. They are also good on crank bolts.

7 Phillips screws crop up on derailleurs and pedals. Check the screwdriver isn't worn and position it in a straight line with the screw before you apply pressure, or it might slip and make it difficult to remove the fixing at all.

8 When metal gets damaged, it's often possible to bend it back again, gripping it in a vice or using a couple of crescent wrenches. But this rearranges all the molecules in the metal and tends to harden it. This work-hardening effect doesn't take place immediately, so try to put the damage right in one go, not a series of separate small adjustments.

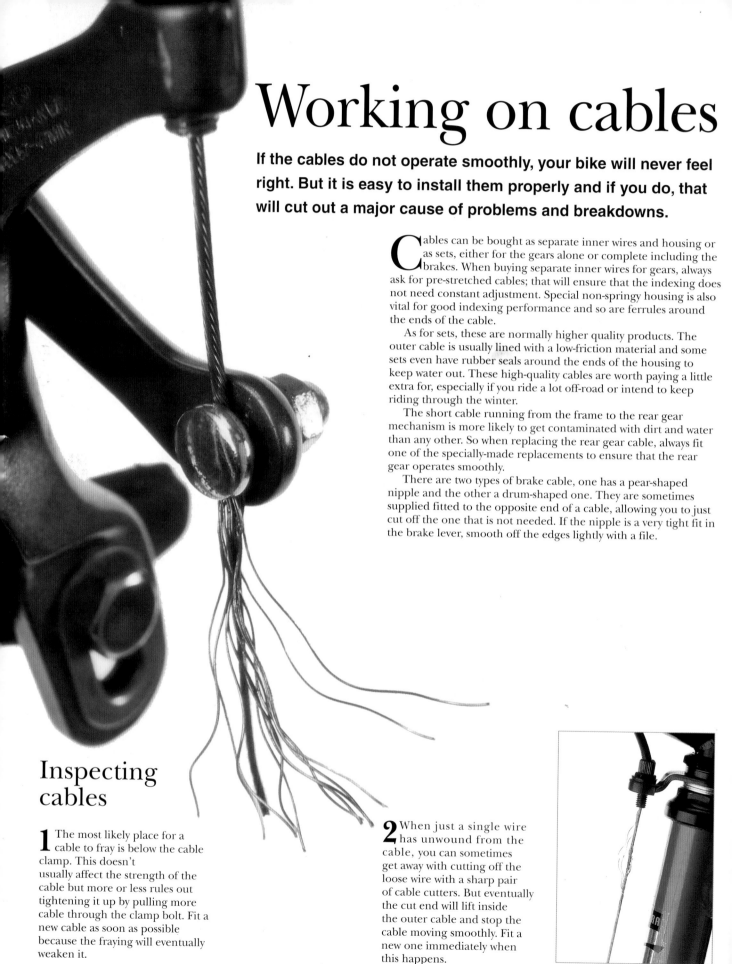

Working on cables

If the cables do not operate smoothly, your bike will never feel right. But it is easy to install them properly and if you do, that will cut out a major cause of problems and breakdowns.

Cables can be bought as separate inner wires and housing or as sets, either for the gears alone or complete including the brakes. When buying separate inner wires for gears, always ask for pre-stretched cables; that will ensure that the indexing does not need constant adjustment. Special non-springy housing is also vital for good indexing performance and so are ferrules around the ends of the cable.

As for sets, these are normally higher quality products. The outer cable is usually lined with a low-friction material and some sets even have rubber seals around the ends of the housing to keep water out. These high-quality cables are worth paying a little extra for, especially if you ride a lot off-road or intend to keep riding through the winter.

The short cable running from the frame to the rear gear mechanism is more likely to get contaminated with dirt and water than any other. So when replacing the rear gear cable, always fit one of the specially-made replacements to ensure that the rear gear operates smoothly.

There are two types of brake cable, one has a pear-shaped nipple and the other a drum-shaped one. They are sometimes supplied fitted to the opposite end of a cable, allowing you to just cut off the one that is not needed. If the nipple is a very tight fit in the brake lever, smooth off the edges lightly with a file.

Inspecting cables

1 The most likely place for a cable to fray is below the cable clamp. This doesn't usually affect the strength of the cable but more or less rules out tightening it up by pulling more cable through the clamp bolt. Fit a new cable as soon as possible because the fraying will eventually weaken it.

2 When just a single wire has unwound from the cable, you can sometimes get away with cutting off the loose wire with a sharp pair of cable cutters. But eventually the cut end will lift inside the outer cable and stop the cable moving smoothly. Fit a new one immediately when this happens.

Cutting standard outer cables

SLOTS AND STOPS

Most recent bikes have slotted cable stops so you can pull out sections of housing without undoing the inner cables. This makes it easier to squirt lubricant down the core of the cable.

1 To cut standard housing, squeeze the cutter lightly so the jaws slide between the coils of wire first. Then squeeze harder to cut the metal part.

2 If the wire cutter leaves a jagged end as on the bottom cable, clean it up with the cutters or a grinder so it's as the top one before fitting.

3 When replacing housing, use the old one as a pattern so you get the length right. Or cut slightly too long and measure against the bike.

4 Ideally, cables should be fitted with a metal ferrule at each end. They protect the plastic outer covering and ensure that the housing seat squarely in the cable stops.

5 Do not try to fit a new inner cable into damaged housing as it will probably start to fray. If this happens, pull the inner cable back and try cutting the damaged end off.

TOOLS FOR WORKING ON CABLES

SIDE CUTTERS
◆ You need a good pair of side cutters before you start replacing cables. Ordinary pliers often include wire cutters but they tend to squash the cable.

SPECIAL CABLE TOOL
◆ Purpose-made cable cutters, as supplied by Shimano and Park among others, work better than side cutters. They work neatly and cleanly on both inner and outer cables.

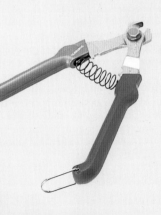

CABLE PULLER
◆ Better than a third-hand tool as they work on gears as well as brakes.

Finishing touches

1 Once you have checked that the derailleur or the brake is working properly, hold the cable taut with one hand while you cut the excess off using a sharp set of cutters.

2 Leave about 2in of spare cable but stop it from fraying by squeezing a cable cap on the end with the lower part of the cutters. Then tuck the end of the cable away neatly.

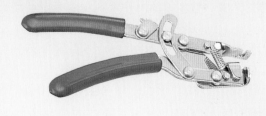

Problem solving

Maybe you have inherited problems with an old bike. Maybe you have fouled up yourself. Luckily most problems can be fixed with a bit of cunning.

Stick to the instructions and advice in this book and, theoretically, you shouldn't have any problems. But sooner or later you will have a crash or forget to apply some anti-seize and you will be in trouble.

To get home after a crash, off-center stems can usually be sorted out if you hold the front wheel between your legs and twist the handlebars. If one side of the handlebars is bent, lay the bike on the ground, place one foot on the other side and pull hard. As always when straightening metal, it's best to exert a slowly increasing amount of force and not make a sudden wrench. If that doesn't work, try to lever the handlebars straight with a length of wood. Once the metal starts to move, don't stop pulling until it's straight. This is only a temporary fix to get you home. These parts should be replace right away.

There are various sorts of problems best left to professionals. A good bike shop can remove seized cranks, straighten bent cranks and extract a corroded seat post. They should also be able to check and correct frame alignment, organize a respray for a frame looking past its best and clean up any damaged threads. If you are fitting a cartridge bottom bracket, some people say you should get the bottom brackets threads recut as a matter of routine. On the other hand, an engineering or engine reconditioning shop would probably be better at dealing with badly-seized nuts and bolts.

Dealing with stuck parts

1 Alloy seat posts can corrode and jam in the frame. If you suspect this has happened, remove the seat bolt and apply penetrating oil around the bottom of the seat post every few hours for a couple of days. Then try again.

2 The best way of getting a grip on a seat post is to bolt on an old saddle. Hit it with a mallet to try to move the seat post. If that doesn't work, try turning it with a strong set of channel locks or a pipe wrench.

5 You always need a long wrench to shift the pedals but if you can not move them, extend the wrench with a tube. However, one of the reasons people have trouble is that they forget the left-hand pedal has a left hand-thread.

3 When a crank or something similar gets stuck, cushion it with cloth or a piece of wood and strike it several times with a hammer. If that doesn't shock it off, try riding a couple of miles with the crank bolt missing.

4 If somebody has tried undoing the wheel nuts with a wrench or used the wrong wrench on the rear derailleur, the best way to undo the damaged nut or bolt is to use a surface drive socket. These grip the sides of the hexagon, not the vulnerable angles.

6 Do not use too much leverage as there is a danger that you will rip the thread out of the crank. Instead, try soaking the threaded part in spray lube. Don't forget the end of the axle where it shows on the inside face of the crank.

7 Sometimes the wrench flats on the pedal axle get damaged. If that happens, dismantle the pedal and clamp the axle in a vice. Then pull on the chainring to unscrew the pedal axle but check you are turning in the right direction.

SAW POINT

If you are desperate, you can sometimes shift obstinate components using a hacksaw. In most cases you will find the junior size best. Fit a new blade before you start to make the whole job easier.

Where something is held in place with a nut and bolt, slip the saw blade in behind the nut and cut through the bolt. If it's very tight for space, you may find yourself cutting through the back of the nut as well but that does not matter. If you are dealing with something like a cable clamp with a damaged Allen socket, cut a deep slot across the socket head and try undoing it with a screwdriver. If you have good access to a nut, try making two diagonal cuts across opposite flats. Then open up the slots with a cold chisel and hammer – the nut will usually fall apart. If all else fails, see if your local machine shop can help.

CHAPTER 3

INSTANT BIKE CARE

Look after your bike and the gears will work better, components will last longer, and you can forget about breakdowns. This chapter tells you everything you need to know about day-to-day maintenance.

Quick lube routine

There are many points that need lubricating on a bike, but most of them need only occasional attention.

A s they rotate, chains tend to throw off any oil you put on them. They also get covered with dust and any oil that clings on gets washed off eventually. But if a chain is allowed to run dry, the chain, chainring, and sprockets all wear out much faster and derailleur gear systems will hardly work at all. The way to prevent this is to lube the chain frequently and to clean it as soon as dirt and dust start to build up on the links. Full instructions on cleaning chains appear on page 74.

For regular commuters, frequently lubing and cleaning the chain means once a week in winter, maybe once every couple of weeks in summer. You should back this up with extra lube for the chain if it has been raining. Leisure riders should lube their bikes after any cross-country trip and soon after any ride over 40 miles on the road.

That leaves the question of when to lube the rest of your bike. If you use this schedule and go through the whole lube routine every time your chain needs attention, your bike certainly won't be under-lubricated but don't let a surplus build-up.

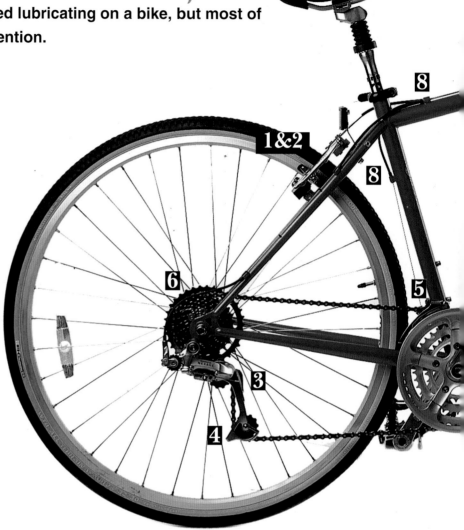

1 V brake pivots are assembled with grease but need a shot of spray lube to keep water and rust at bay. Give the cable attachments a very occasional shot as well.

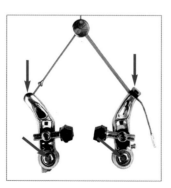

2 Standard cantilevers also need a shot of lube to protect the pivots and just a trace to ensure that the straddle cable does not seize or fray where it joins the brake arms.

3 Rear derailleurs need a shot of lube on each of the main pivots, the top pivot and the chain cage pivot. In other words–if it moves, spray it but only lightly.

4 Jockey wheel bearings do not pick up oil from the chain, so they need a long squirt to shift any dirt, a wipe, and maybe a second shot to keep them turning smoothly.

BRUSH OFF

When using your bike in dry weather, dust collects in all the nooks and crannies. If you do not have time to wash the bike before starting the lube routine, brush off all the dust with a paint brush but be careful to keep it away from the chain. This prevents any abrasive dust from being carried into the chain bushes and inner links along with the oil.

WHICH LUBRICANT?

There is a never-ending procession of new and ever more expensive bike lubricants trying to find room in bike shops. The problem is that nobody can tell right away if the new ones are any better than the old, let alone whether it is worth shelling out for the really expensive ones. Unless you enjoy trying new things and do not mind a bike shed full of half-empty cans, it is probably best to stick to products that have been around at least a couple of years. At least that proves somebody else thinks they are worth the money.

5 The front derailleur needs a squirt on all the pivots, then a quick wipe around the chain cage. Lube the outside of the gear shifters and also wherever the inner cable makes a bend.

6 Lubricating the chain and sprockets is the highest priority, but the chainring also needs attention if it is dirty or dry. Lube inside the short cable housing as well.

7 The brake levers need a quick shot on the pivots, on the cable with the lever pulled back, and around the cable adjusters. At the same time, check the brake pads for wear.

8 Give all inner cables a squirt where they exit from the cable housing, but remove the cable from the stop and fire lube down it if the action is at all heavy or the roads are wet.

Big clean-up

Mountain bikes always need a good scrub down after a muddy ride but any sort of bike looks brighter after a thorough wash and polish.

The obvious thing to wash your bike with is dish washing liquid. That's fine if it is really oily because any strong detergent will strip most of the oil off, along with any wax or polish on the frame. But the frame will probably look streaky because of the phosphates left behind. You will have to shine it up with car polish if you want to put the gleam back.

If you find areas where the liquid is not cutting through the dirt, apply a spot of degreaser, agitate with a paint brush, and then wash again.

If your bike is just normally dirty, you might do better to wash it in car shampoo. This is generally less aggressive and does not leave streaks.

Try to avoid washing your bike in the sun because the heat will dry the frame too quickly, increasing the chances of streaks.

Keep the bike upright, standing on its wheels, but never use a pressure washer. Bike bearings are just not designed to keep out water under pressure. You can use a hose but keep the pressure down, hold it over the bike, and do not squirt it directly at the hubs, bottom bracket, gears, or headset.

Cleaning kit

SPRAY LUBE

SPRAY DEGREASER

BRUSH-ON DEGREASER

LIQUID SOAP

1 Squirt plenty of soap or a packet of automotive wash into half a bucket of hot water. Apply a first coat to the whole bike using an old sponge or soft scrub brush but give it time to work.

2 Wash the whole bike again. This second wash will shift most of the dirt, but there may be areas where the dirt is more stubborn. Use a bottle brush or old tooth brush to get into the nooks and crannies.

WHEN YOU NEED TO DO THIS JOB
◆ After a cross-country ride.
◆ Every two or three months.

TIME
◆ Half an hour to do the job properly. Ten minutes if you're in a real hurry.

DIFFICULTY
◆ Dead easy. There is no excuse for not keeping your bike gleaming.

SPECIAL TOOLS
◆ Bottle brush, washing-up brush, toothbrush, close-textured sponge, chamois leather.

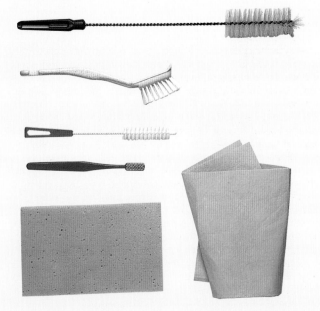

3 Wherever the foam seems to form droplets and roll off, use a squirt of degreaser to break down the film of oil. Do the same to the chain. Use an old paint brush to ensure the dirt mixes with the degreaser.

4 If you have plenty of time, get a bucket of clean warm water and rinse the foam away. Use a sponge to cascade water over the frame, the fenders, and the chain. But use it gently or it will get torn to pieces.

5 Dry the frame, fenders, saddle, and handlebars with a clean rag or a chamois. Then squirt spray lube over areas like the chain, gears, and hubs where water might penetrate the mechanism.

WASH, LUBE, AND GO
When you have finished washing your bike, even if you have dried it quite carefully, there is still a chance that water will have got into the bearings. On the other hand, if you oil your bike without washing it, there is a chance that dirt will get into the bearings. So treat washing and lubing as two parts of the one job and allow about an hour for the combined effort.

10-minute bike check

This routine will help you assess whether your bike is in good enough shape for daily commuting or a ride in the country.

The first three steps in this test routine cover the brakes. If you find any defects, do not use your bike until you have put things right as you are a danger to yourself and other road users until then. As for the other faults, most of them should not stop you from riding but there is always the risk of damaging the bike or having to walk home.

Next come checks on steering. It will be fairly obvious if anything is out of line but not so easy to tell if the headset is loose or worn. However, if you hear or feel a jolt when you lunge the bike forward and then apply the front brake, the headset almost certainly needs adjusting. Iif there is only a little slack, you might find it easier to detect if you wedge your finger between the frame and the fork. Adjust or replace as soon as possible because loose headsets wear fast.

The drivetrain comes next. If you can detect movement on just one crank or the cranks feel tight or gritty when you turn them, it is best not to ride until the problem is fixed. It is OK to ride with a loose bottom bracket but it will slow you down–so will a bent chainring and bent cranks.

Gear cables tend to fray in similar places to brake cables, but they also fray under the bottom bracket on road bikes. However, badly adjusted rear derailleurs are the main cause of unreliability on nearly all bikes. So check that there is a quick reliable change between all gears. If the chain jumps off at any point, you will have to adjust the rear derailleur from scratch. Check the indexing as well–changes should be crisp and instantaneous.

Finally, check that the bolts on the saddle clip, the seat post clamp and the handlebar stem are all tight. Avoid overtightening them because it is only too easy to damage alloy components.

Ideally, do your 10-minute check before the Quick Lube routine but after the Big Clean-Up on earlier pages. That way you will be working on a clean, but not oily, bike. However, leave time for the lube routine when you have finished the checks.

1 If the brakes are properly adjusted, they will be fully on by the time you've pulled the lever about halfway to the handlebars. It is a danger signal if you can pull the brake lever any closer than that.

5 If there is any headset movement, fix it fast. Then go around checking that the clamp bolts on the stem, handlebars, and handlebar brace are all tight. Check also that any exposed bolts on suspension forks are tight.

9 On the rear derailleur, check the cable for fraying near the cable clamp and wiggle the jockey wheels to see if they are worn. Shift from top gear to bottom and back a few times to check that the gear change is swift and accurate.

2 You must check the brake pads next. There should be plenty of rubber left and 2mm or slightly less between the pad and the top edge of the rim. Curved pads should follow the curve of the rim.

3 Check the brake cables for fraying near the cable adjusters and where they exit from the cable housing. Check also if it takes a lot of pressure to fully apply the brakes. Fit new cables if necessary.

4 Check the handlebars and stem for cracks and that the stem lines up with the front wheel. Then apply the front brake and see if you can hear any movement in the headset or feel any with your fingers.

6 Hold one of the cranks still and try to move the other one. Then swap around. If you feel any movement on one of the cranks, the crank bolts need tightening. If the cranks move the same amount on both sides, the bottom bracket needs adjusting.

7 Lift the chain off the chainrings so you can turn the cranks freely. If necessary, take out the back wheel to give you enough slack in the chain to pull it clear. Then rotate the cranks to see if the bottom bracket turns smoothly.

8 While the chain is off, look down from above to see if the cranks and the chainrings are both straight. Then check that all the chainring bolts are tight. Finally, make sure the pedals revolve freely, without any cracking noises.

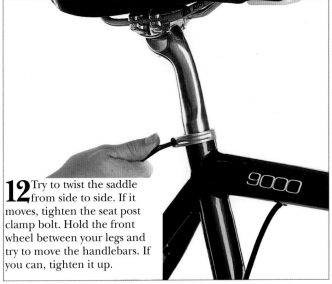

10 Inspect the front derailleur cable for fraying and make sure the chain cage is parallel to the chain. Then check that there is a 1- to 3-mm gap between chain cage and chainring. The change itself should be quick and reliable.

11 Check that the riding position is comfortable and that your leg is almost fully extended when pedaling. Then tighten the seat clip bolt or bolts but take care not to over-tighten them because the alloy threads are easily damaged.

12 Try to twist the saddle from side to side. If it moves, tighten the seat post clamp bolt. Hold the front wheel between your legs and try to move the handlebars. If you can, tighten it up.

Wheel and tire servicing

Do this 5-minute check on your wheels and tires at the same time as the 10-minute check on the previous page.

When you spin the front wheel, it should keep on turning for quite a while and there should not be any kind of grinding or cracking noise. If it seems to slow quite quickly or you can hear odd noises, the hub probably needs stripping down and regreasing. If you can feel any side to side movement at the rim, the hub bearings need adjusting – see page 134.

As the wheel turns, use the brake pads to check if the wheel rim appears to move from side to side or up and down. If you can see that the rim is buckled, see page 136. In addition, all the spokes in a wheel should be at roughly the same tension. If there is a buckle, some of the spokes will probably be loose, but if they all seem to be slack, the wheel needs complete re-tensioning by a professional bike mechanic.

No tire runs absolutely true, but if the tread seems to wander from side to side a lot, try taking it off and refitting it more carefully. On the other hand, if that does not improve things, the tread of the tire may have been manufactured crooked or there may be a bulge in the side wall. In both these cases, the only solution is a new tire.

When you are checking the tire tread for flints, look also for sponginess, deep cuts, and an excessive number of cuts. If there are more than a dozen or so cuts, the tire is coming to the end of its days.

5-minute tire and wheel check

1 Lift the front wheel off the ground and give it a spin to check the hub bearings. Then use the brake pads as a fixed point to see if the rim or tire is not running straight. Try to gauge how bad the problem is.

BUBBLE TROUBLE

If a tire keeps going down but you cannot find the puncture, the valve may be slowly leaking air. This will show up if you remove the tube and dunk it in water, but there is a way of checking without going that far. Just fill an egg cup or yogurt pot with water and dip the valve in. If there is a stream of bubbles, you will have to install a new tube if it is a Presta valve, or a new insert if it is a Schrader.

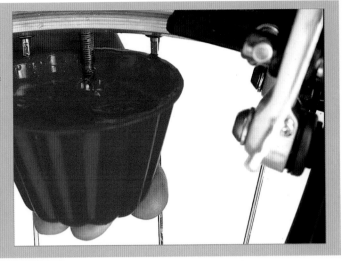

2 If the tire isn't running straight, take it off and re-fit it, fitting the beads right into the well of the rim. Then, whether it is buckled or not, stretch each pair of spokes with your finger and thumb to see if they are evenly tensioned.

3 Go around the tire with a small screwdriver next, prying out any flints stuck in the tread. Look out for deep cuts, whether or not there is a flint embedded in them, and consider fitting a new tire if there is any serious damage.

4 The tire wall should be evenly colored, with an unbroken coat of rubber all the way from the rim to the tread. If the fabric is showing or there are any cuts or splits, let the tire down so you can see how bad the damage is.

5 Round off this check by turning the axle with your fingers. It should feel smooth, but if it is tight or gritty, strip and regrease. If it feels smooth, lay the wheel flat, clean around the axle, and run a few drops of oil into the bearings.

Inflating tires

1 To pump up a Presta valve, undo the knurled nut all the way and push in the stalk until you hear a hiss of escaping air. This ensures that the valve is not stuck but you may have to wiggle the stalk if it is hard to pump up the tire.

2 A few mountain and utility bikes have a Schrader valve, which is a bit fatter than a Presta. Some pumps fit both types but you may need an adapter, so check. Don't use garage air lines on Schrader valves–it is dangerous.

3 Most pumps just push onto the valve, but the air will escape if you push the adapter on too far. If you are having trouble, check that the adapter is square onto the valve and steady your hand with a finger around the valve or a spoke.

4 When you have fully inflated a tire with a Presta valve, check that the valve is at right angles to the rim and that the valve nut is finger tight. Don't tighten it more than that as it might cause the valve to leak. Then refit the dust cap.

10 hard-to-spot faults

After doing the 10-minute bike check, you should have enough know-how to spot most common problems. This page is to help you pick out more unusual faults.

The 10-minute bike check will tell you if your bike is basically sound or not. But it will not help you trace the minor niggling problems that make the difference between a bike that is marginal and one that is a pleasure to ride. Once you have spotted one of the problems outlined here, read the section covering that area to get a better idea about what action is needed.

First of all, do not neglect your riding position. Most people just get the saddle height approximately right and leave it at that. They forget the other saddle adjustments, the possible need to install a different saddle, as well as arm reach and handlebar width. Look back to page 12 for guidance on this point.

The biggest source of problems is the gears. If they are not working properly and minor adjustments don't sort things out, go back and rework the adjustment from scratch. If that does not work, you will have to install a new chain, sprockets, and possibly new chainrings and a new derailleur.

You may also have to splash out on some new tires. Just because there is a millimeter of tread left, it does not mean that the sidewalls are in roadworthy condition. Good-quality tires are the easiest and best upgrade for any bike—you will even go faster if you keep them properly pumped up.

The better the bike, the more likely it is that you will come across various creaking noises, because they are caused by different metals rubbing together. Do not try to eliminate them by overtightening bolts because there is a chance you will rip the thread out. Undo them and coat everything with anti-seize grease.

Brakes next. Again, just because there is a millimeter of rubber left on the pad, it does not mean that the pad is gripping the rim properly. Adjust them so that they toe-in slightly at the front— see page 118, although the new pads may well have instructions covering this point. Do not expect the new pads to generate full power immediately—the pads usually have to lay a coating of the new material on the rims and wear into the shape of the braking surface before they reach full power.

Finally, there are the forgotten bearings. If a bike is getting older you may find that these components are just worn out.

1 Too much effort needed, discomfort, aches and pains, or a feeling of poor control over the bike can all be caused by a bad riding position. Go back to the basic set up in Chapter 1 and work from there.

2 The chain is worn if you can almost lift it off the chainring. It won't cause clear-cut problems, but the chainrings and sprockets will wear fast and the gear change will be sloppy and inaccurate.

5 Tires may look good from a distance, but it takes a close examination to get at the truth. If a tire wall looks past it, try letting the tire down so you can squeeze it flat and check for splits and cuts.

6 Bikes should be silent. If yours creaks, the noise probably comes from steel bolts in alloy threads or vice versa. Apply anti-seize to the stem, chain wheel, and saddle clamp bolts to silence them.

3 If there is a regular noise that stops when you stop pedaling, the indexing on the rear derailleur is probably inaccurate. Try turning the cable adjuster on the rear gear one half turn counterclockwise.

4 You can prevent the chain jumping off the sprockets by readjusting the rear derailleur from scratch. If that does not fix things, check the chain isn't too long. When the chain is on the biggest sprocket and the biggest chainring, the chain cage should be at an angle of roughly 45° to the floor.

Front

7 Poor braking may be due to contaminated brake pads. Try fitting new ones. If there seems to be a build up on the rim, scrub the rims using a green nylon abrasive pad and some degreaser.

8 Snatchy and noisy braking can be caused by badly fitted brake pads, especially if each pad is aligned differently. Try fitting them so that the front edge is 1mm closer to the rim than the back edge.

9 To check the headset for freeplay, wrap your fingers around the top steering bearing, put the front brake on, and rock backward and forward. Any movement means the headset must be checked.

10 Pedals with grinding bearings or bent axles make it impossible to pedal correctly. Check that the axle is straight by eye, then spin the pedal so that you can check how the bearings are.

CHAPTER 4

GEAR SYSTEMS

Where drivers see a flat road, bike riders see climbs and dips. When weather forecasters talk about a still day, cyclists can still feel the wind. We know that every day and every road is different, each requiring a different gear ratio to strike a balance between speed and effort.

Types of gears

Nearly all bikes are fitted with either derailleur or hub gears. Derailleurs have a front derailleur to shift the chain between two or three chainrings at the front and a rear derailleur for up to ten sprockets at the back. These gears need a lot of minor maintenance but they are light, efficient, and suit most conditions. Hub gears have three, four, five, or seven speeds and need occasional workshop maintenance.

NINE SPEED MOUNTAIN BIKE REAR DERAILLEUR
The long chain cage allows for a very wide range of gears, usually controlled by a handlebar gear shifter. Also used on hybrid and touring bikes, this particular type is partly molded from a high-strength composite material.

REAR DERAILLEUR

NINE SPEED RACING BIKE REAR DERAILLEUR
Has a short chain cage for low weight and a better gear change. Controlled by a shifter on the down tube of the frame or STI/Ergopower combined brake and gear levers.

ECONOMY REAR DERAILLEUR
Made of steel, with a bolt-on hanger for use on frames without a gear hanger. Short cage model also available.

HUB GEARS
With optional built-in coaster brake. Designed as low-maintenance gears for city bikes. Controlled by click shifter on handlebars. Need little adjustment. Up to seven speeds are available.

HUB GEAR

THREE-SPEED HUB GEARS
For utility bikes. Need occasional adjustment to the cable tension, but latest versions do not need oiling. Click shifter usually on the handlebars.

FRONT DERAILLEUR

MOUNTAIN BIKE AND HYBRID FRONT DERAILLEUR
Deep chain cage for use with triple chainrings, with big differences in the number of teeth. This particular type has a very rigid chain cage mounted at the top of the derailleur for a lighter, better change. Top pull models with the cable pulling upwards and bottom pull models with the cable pulling downward are both available.

RACING BIKE FRONT DERAILLEUR
Fitted with a light chain cage, separate models are now available for double and triple chainrings. Most types bolt on to the down tube with a clip, but high-grade road frames have a special brazed-on fitting for bolting the front derailleur to.

Rear derailleur: care and inspection

When you are climbing a hill and the pedals are going round slower and slower, you need a quick change-down to a lower gear. This is the big test for any rear derailleur.

The rear derailleur is the most important part of a derailleur gear system and needs regular lubrication and attention. However, that does not mean every week – every month is more like it. To find out exactly what to do, you need to know whether or not the rear derailleur is indexed.

If you have an older bike, it will probably have friction gears. With these, you have to judge how far to move the gear lever each time you want to change gear. Nevertheless, once you have got the hang of it, each change should be crisp and each gear should come in with one clank only.

Most bikes now have indexed gears, including the latest 10-speed systems, so you will feel and hear a click as you move the gear lever, along with a slight answering clank as the chain jumps onto the chosen sprocket. Index gears are usually fitted with a top jockey wheel that moves from side to side a little. So the jockey wheels do not have to be exactly in line with the sprocket, which allows for any slight inaccuracies in the adjustment of the cable.

If either type of rear derailleur throws the chain off the sprockets, or you can detect the continuous metallic rattling sound of the chain trying to move onto the next sprocket but not quite making it, something is wrong. The first steps to putting this right are cleaning, lubing, and adjusting, as explained in the next few pages.

REMEMBER: Bottom and the rest of the low gears are for climbing hills. Top and the other high gears are for descents.

AT THE BACK WHEEL, the small sprocket is top gear, the large sprocket is bottom.

BUT ON THE CRANKSET, the small ring is bottom gear, the big ring is top gear.

1 If you have had to clean the chain, the rear derailleur probably needs cleaning as well. Give it a squirt of aerosol lube or grease solvent and wipe it thoroughly with a cloth. Then lube all the main pivots, plus the top pivot bolt.

2 Pay particular attention to the jockey wheels because they pick up hard-packed dirt off the chain. Soften the dirt with solvent and scrape off with a small screwdriver. Wipe, and then fire lube into the center of both jockey wheels.

4 The jockey wheels wear out more quickly than any other part. To check, pull the chain cage forward to free the bottom jockey from the chain, then test for movement by trying to wiggle it. Check also that the jockey wheel turns freely.

5 Pull the chain away from the upper jockey wheel next and do the same check. On most indexed derailleurs, the top jockey wheel must move sideways a bit, so try to tell the difference between wear and this intentional movement.

WHEN YOU NEED TO DO THIS JOB:
◆ Steps 1, 2, and 3 – every time you lube the chain.
◆ Steps 4, 5, and 6 – every time you give the chain a thorough cleaning. It's also worth going through 4, 5, and 6 when checking over a second-hand bike.

TIME:
◆ 1 minute to lube the rear derailleur when you do the chain. 5 minutes to check wear and crash damage.

DIFFICULTY:
◆ Quite easy, but you are liable to get your hands dirty. Consider wearing latex gloves.

3 The cable should instantly transmit each movement of the gear lever. To make sure it does work like this, lubricate the inner cable, then operate the gear lever a few times so that the lube works its way right down the outer cable.

6 Hanging down beside the back wheel, rear derailleurs are quite liable to damage when a bike falls over, whether you are on it or not. To check for damage, clamp the bike in a workstand or get somebody to hold it upright. Then position yourself behind the back wheel, with your eye level with the hub. From here you will be able to see if the gear looks out of line with the frame. If you suspect that it is, check the gear hanger for signs of cracks or chips in the paint— a sure indication that it is bent. It is also worth checking that the chain cage plates look straight. If all is well, the top and bottom jockey wheels will line up exactly with the sprockets.

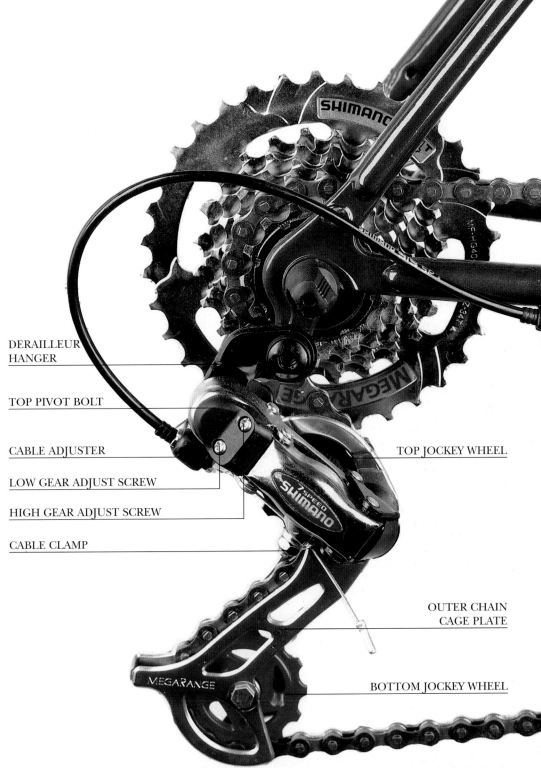

DERAILLEUR HANGER

TOP PIVOT BOLT

CABLE ADJUSTER

LOW GEAR ADJUST SCREW

HIGH GEAR ADJUST SCREW

CABLE CLAMP

TOP JOCKEY WHEEL

OUTER CHAIN CAGE PLATE

BOTTOM JOCKEY WHEEL

EXTRA-LOW GEARING

Setting a new design trend, Mega-range gears work with a bottom sprocket that has no less than 34 teeth. It can only cope because the derailleur is mounted slightly further back than usual and has a unique, 13 tooth bottom jockey wheel. This extra-large jockey wheel has to be used to cope with the extra long chain. Mega-range gears are also Rapid Rise, so go to page 52 for special instructions on adjustment.

Rear derailleur adjustment: Shimano and Campagnolo

If your rear derailleur is indexed, you may have to go through all six steps to get the gear change right. But only the first four steps apply to old-style friction derailleurs.

The basic adjustment of an indexed rear derailleur and a friction one is identical. You just have to make sure that the chain cage does not move too far in either direction, otherwise the chain will tend to jam in the spokes or between the top sprocket and the frame. But only the first four steps apply to friction derailleurs. After that, you just have to tinker with the H and L screws (small arrows) to get the adjustment absolutely correct.

There are also important differences between the two types. On friction derailleurs, the cable only has to be tightened up or changed occasionally. On index gears, the click mechanism in the gear lever controls the movement of the cable, and this set amount of movement must be transmitted to the rear derailleur very accurately. To achieve this, the inner gear cable has to be kept under exactly the same amount of tension at all times.

Once you have got the indexing working well, it is usually enough to give the cable adjuster one half-turn counter-clockwise if it plays up. When that does not work, try another half turn counter-clockwise. If all is still not well, go through step 6 below.

When you have to keep fiddling with the cable adjustment or just can not get the gears to change smoothly and precisely, install a new inner and outer gear cable.

See the next page for SRAM, Gripshift and Shimano Rapid Rise adjustment.

Indexing adjustment

6 When adjusting the indexing from scratch on Shimano, check that the chain runs silently in top gear. If it doesn't, turn the cable adjuster (large arrow)—not the H and L adjuster – one turn counter-clockwise if the chain is trying to jump off the top sprocket, and one turn clockwise if it's trying to climb onto the second sprocket. Adjusting the cable tension in this way has a similar effect to adjusting the H adjuster on the gear.

Next, change down to second gear with the gear lever and turn the cable adjuster half a turn counter-clockwise at a time, until you hear a metallic clattering sound as the chain tries to climb onto the third sprocket. Then turn the adjuster clockwise until the clattering noise stops, but absolutely no further than that. Road test to check that you get quick, accurate changes between all gears.

Campagnolo, Sachs, and Suntour indexing is adjusted in a similar way, but with the rear derailleur in top and second gear rather than second and third.

Basic adjustment: friction and index

1 If you are adjusting friction gears, make sure that the center screw of the shifter is fairly tight. On some index gears, both down tube and handlebar shifters, there is a choice between friction and indexed gear changing. Check now that the center screw or indicator is firmly switched to the indexed position.

2 Check that the inner cable is well lubricated and not frayed at all, particularly near the rear derailleur. And that the outer cable is not kinked or broken. Replace where necessary. Now lift the back wheel and select top gear, turning the pedals slowly so that the chain jumps down on to the smallest sprocket.

3 Undo the cable clamp to free the gear cable, then pull the rear derailleur backwards into a vertical position. That makes it easier to see the position of the jockey wheels. On index gears, a vertical line through the middle of both jockey wheels should line up with the outer edge of the smallest sprocket. But on a friction gear, they should line up with the middle of the sprocket. To move the jockey wheels to the right, turn the H for High adjuster counterclockwise. To move the jockey wheels to the left, turn it clockwise, the opposite way.

4 Still working from behind, push the rear derailleur sideways with your right hand, then lift the chain onto the bottom sprocket with your left. The jockey wheels should line up with the middle of the bottom sprocket. If they do not, turn the L adjuster clockwise if the chain cage is to the left of the largest sprocket, and counter-clockwise if it lies to the right. Now lift the saddle so you can give the pedals a few quick turns. The chain should quickly jump down to the smallest sprocket and stay there.

5 If you have trouble finding the H (top) and L (bottom) adjusters, they are usually on the top or back of the rear derailleur but on budget Shimano and most Campagnolo gears, they are on the side, near the cable clamp. If they are not labeled H and L, you will have to experiment to find which one is which.

Next, check that the gear lever is still in top gear position. Then screw in the cable adjuster most of the way and reinstall the gear cable, pulling it taut with pliers before tightening the cable clamp. Road test friction gears at this point, making fine adjustments to the H and L screws if the chain runs noisily in either top or bottom gear.

If you are working on an indexed rear derailleur, go now to step six on the opposite page.

Remember, at the back wheel:
The smaller the sprocket, the higher the gear. So adjust the screw marked H for High.
The larger the sprocket, the lower the gear. So adjust the screw marked L for Low.
But at the chainwheel:
The larger the chainring, the higher the gear. So adjust the screw marked H for High.
The smaller the chainring, the lower the gear. So adjust the screw marked L for Low.

WHEN YOU NEED TO DO THIS JOB
◆ Rear derailleur is noisy.
◆ Gears won't change smoothly and accurately.
◆ Chain jumps off into spokes or jams between sprocket and frame.

TIME
◆ 30 minutes from fitting new derailleur to completing adjustment of indexed rear derailleur.
◆ 5 minutes to fine-tune the indexing, including test ride.

DIFFICULTY
◆ Basic adjustment is quite straightforward, but getting the indexing working perfectly can take a bit of patience.

Rear derailleur adjustment: SRAM & Shimano Rapid Rise

There are important differences between the way you adjust these two types of rear derailleur and the mainstream types. Nevertheless, it is worth reading the previous spread before starting this one to get an understanding of the basics of rear derailleur adjustment.

Shimano Rapid Rise rear derailleurs work the other way around from all other types. That means the rear derailleur automatically moves into bottom gear when the tension on the cable is released and not into top gear as on all other types. This is claimed to be an advantage because it is always harder to get the chain to climb up onto a larger sprocket than to drop down onto a smaller one. With the Rapid Rise design, the more difficult down change is assisted by the pull of the spring and not hindered by it, as on other designs.

SRAM ESP-type gears also work on a very different principle from others—they call it the 1:1 actuation ratio. With this design, if you pull the cable 1 mm, the rear derailleur moves 1 mm. On all other designs, moving the cable 1mm moves the rear derailleur 2 mm, which means that the cable must be adjusted very accurately. The 1:1 ratio also does away with the need for the top jockey wheel to move from side to side. It is claimed that the practical effect of all this is that SRAM gears do not need such frequent maintenance as other types and that the indexing works much more reliably.

SRAM gear

1 Provided the chain is the correct length (see page 78 for details) adjust the H screw so that a line between the centers of the jockey wheels lines up with the outer edge of the smallest sprocket.

Rapid Rise adjustment

1 When the cable tension is off, a Rapid Rise gear automatically moves the chain onto the largest sprocket. So start the process off by turning the pedals until the chain is on the biggest sprocket.

2 Adjust the L screw so that the jockey wheels sit in line with the inner (wheel) edge of the largest sprocket. Then tighten the cable adjuster until the chain runs quietly on the biggest sprocket.

RAPID RISE
The Shimano Rapid Rise concept first came onto the market at the top of the MTB range. The early version had a complex pulley mechanism on the cable but this has now been eliminated. On the other hand, the budget Nexave leisure bike component group also has a Rapid Rise rear derailleur, so maybe this design will appear on all Shimano rear derailleurs.

SRAM FRONT DERAILLEUR
The SRAM front derailleur is much more conventional than the rear derailleur. Adjustment is covered on page 58, but the chain cage should be located even closer to the chainring than the other makes. Some versions of the SRAM shifter work with both top and bottom pull cables.

adjustment

2 Turn the pedals with one hand while you push the rear derailleur towards the bottom sprocket with the other. Once the chain is on the biggest sprocket, hold the derailleur in that position and adjust the L screw so that the jockey wheels line up precisely with the biggest sprocket.

3 Holding the gear in the same position, count the number of chain rivets between the point where the chain leaves the biggest sprocket and where it contacts the top jockey wheel. Adjust the 'B' screw until there are exactly three rivets between them. This adjustment is not so significant on other makes, but it is very important on SRAM. Complete the adjustment process using the same method as any other gear derailleur.

4 To change the cable, flip off the cover beside the cable adjuster. Then cut the old cable and push it out through the cable entry. Insert the new cable and feed it through the cable entry, the adjuster, and along the outer cable. When it emerges, pull the rest through, make sure it lies in the cable track, and snap the cover back on. For top of the range models, push back the escape hatch near the adjuster, undo the 2.5 mm socket-headed cable retainer inside and push the old cable out. Feed the new cable in, pull it tight, and reinstall the cable retainer.

5 Install the new cable on the rear derailleur in the normal way. But if a Nightcrawler cable seal is installed, feed the new cable through the pointed end of the long rubber bellows first, next the rubber seal, then the small nozzle of the plastic rigger. Continue feeding the inner cable through the second rubber seal and into the normal outer cable. Snap the rigger onto the cable stop and push all the parts together to form a continuous waterproof seal. Again, install the new cable to the rear derailleur in the usual way.

SRAM REAR DERAILLEUR
These rear derailleurs are only made for MTBs and hybrids. The main body of the gear is twisted slightly so that the jockey wheels and chain cage follow the profile of the sprockets as it changes up and down. In addition, the top part of the gear does not have a spring, as other designs do.

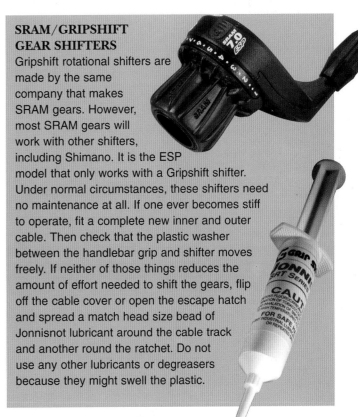

SRAM/GRIPSHIFT GEAR SHIFTERS
Gripshift rotational shifters are made by the same company that makes SRAM gears. However, most SRAM gears will work with other shifters, including Shimano. It is the ESP model that only works with a Gripshift shifter. Under normal circumstances, these shifters need no maintenance at all. If one ever becomes stiff to operate, fit a complete new inner and outer cable. Then check that the plastic washer between the handlebar grip and shifter moves freely. If neither of those things reduces the amount of effort needed to shift the gears, flip off the cable cover or open the escape hatch and spread a match head size bead of Jonnisnot lubricant around the cable track and another round the ratchet. Do not use any other lubricants or degreasers because they might swell the plastic.

Rear derailleur:

If you have carefully adjusted your rear derailleur but still cannot get the gears working nicely, it may need cleaning and rebuild.

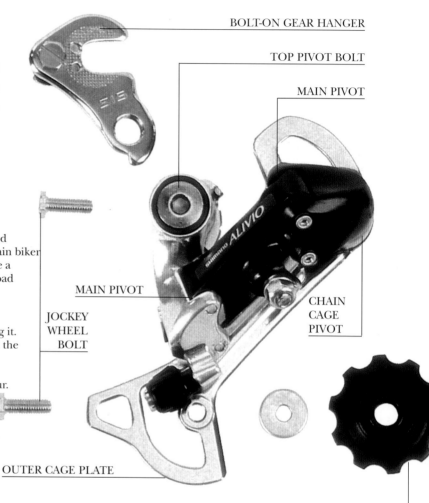

BOLT-ON GEAR HANGER

TOP PIVOT BOLT

MAIN PIVOT

MAIN PIVOT

JOCKEY WHEEL BOLT

CHAIN CAGE PIVOT

OUTER CAGE PLATE

BOTTOM JOCKEY WHEEL

There is no set amount of time or number of kilometers at which you should strip down and clean a rear derailleur. So the kind of mountain biker who revels in muddy tracks might need to do it once a month, or even sooner. On the other hand, many road riders leave the gears untouched for years.

That is leaving it too long. During that time, the jockey wheels will probably start to seize up and the gear change will deteriorate, all without you noticing it. To prevent this from happening, you should inspect the jockey wheels whenever you lubricate the chain. If there is a noticeable build-up of dirt on the jockey wheels, it is time to strip and clean the rear derailleur.

Most gears break down into more parts than shown in the diagram. But there is seldom any need to go further than separating the chain cage plates and the jockey wheels. Remember that jockey wheels sometimes have deeper washers on one side than the other and make a note of which side they fit. The remaining parts like the springs and H and L adjusters can usually be cleaned with solvent, while still in place.

That leaves the question of how badly worn the rear derailleur is. To check, while the derailleur is still on the bike, hold the bottom of the chain cage with two fingers and see how far it moves without being forced. If it moves more than 5 mm or so, investigate further.

This is done by stripping the derailleur and gripping it above and below the two main pivots. Then see if you can feel any movement or play between the top part of the gear and the bottom part. The movement you are trying to detect is parallel with the bike wheels. Do not confuse this with the normal sideways motion. If you can feel more than the slightest amount of play, install a new derailleur. This is shown on page 56.

The method of removing the rear derailleur from the frame shown here avoids splitting the chain It should be used whenever possible. This is because when you break the chain apart, you introduce a weakness. Nevertheless, if you find you cannot undo the jockey wheel bolts, you will have to split the chain using a chain tool and then unbolt the rear derailleur. This method is shown on page 56.

Clean and dry all the parts thoroughly before re-assembly. And remember that the top jockey wheel is usually designed to move from side to side a little. So if the pulley is marked 'Centron' or has a metal bushing molded into it, it is the top jockey roller. Half-fill the center of both jockey wheels with waterproof grease, before putting the washers in place. And use anti-seize grease on the jockey wheel bolts to make sure it is easy to undo them in the future.

Removing a rear derailleur

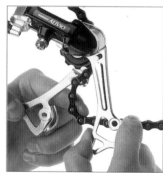

1 Undo the bolt holding the bottom jockey wheel in the chain cage and lift it away. Try to keep the washers in place on the jockey wheel. If the bolt will not shift, soak the head and the other end with spray lube and try again later.

2 Loosen the top jockey bolt next, which should allow you to swing the inner cage plate away. Then pull the chain away from the top jockey wheel and lift it onto one of the large sprockets. Let the slack hang down.

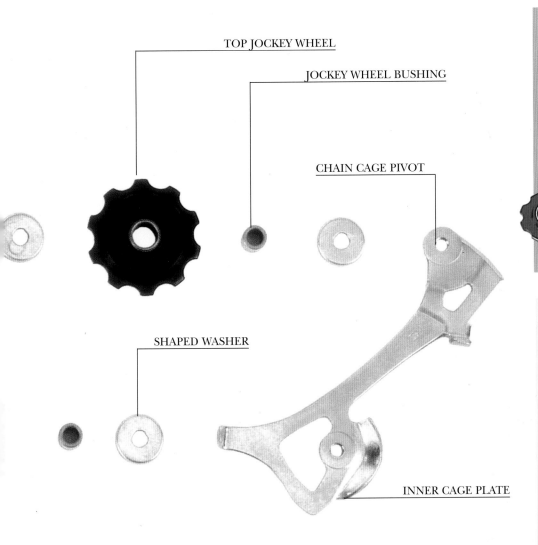

TOP JOCKEY WHEEL

JOCKEY WHEEL BUSHING

CHAIN CAGE PIVOT

SHAPED WASHER

INNER CAGE PLATE

SEALED JOCKEY WHEELS

If the jockey wheels are worn, you have a choice between using spares from the maker, or fitting sealed jockey wheels with proper ball bearings from another supplier. These will last longer and need less maintenance, though they are around twice the price.

WHEN YOU NEED TO DO THIS JOB:
◆ Poor changing indicates derailleur needs cleaning.
◆ Inspection reveals jockey wheels are worn.

TIME:
◆ About 1 hour to remove, thoroughly clean and reinstall a rear derailleur.

DIFFICULTY
◆ It's sometimes hard to reassemble the jockey wheels correctly. Try making a drawing as you take the chain cage apart so you do not mix up the various washers and bushes.

SPECIAL TOOLS
◆ It is very important to have a well-fitting wrench or hex key to undo the jockey wheel bolts.

3 The rear derailleur is now ready for removal. Pry away the plastic cover over the top pivot bolt, or clean out the socket. Then undo the pivot bolt with a hex key. You may have to pull the derailleur away from the chain.

4 When you have removed the rear derailleur, place it on a work surface and clean thoroughly with solvent applied with an old tooth brush, then water. Use anti-seize grease on the pivot bolt when re-installing the derailleur to the frame.

5 On most of the more expensive rear derailleurs, the chain cage is held together with socket head bolts countersunk into the cage plates. This is no different from the bolted designs, but it does require extra care when dismantling.

Rear derailleur: removal and re-installing

Removing and re-installing an old derailleur or installing a new one brings together various skills. In particular, do not forget to set the length of the chain correctly.

There are three different ways in which the rear derailleur is fitted to the frame. In the one shown on page 54 and here, the top pivot bolt screws directly into a threaded hanger on the rear end. This is mainly found on good, quality bikes.

The only problem that can arise during fitting is if you try to screw the pivot bolt in at an angle. If you do this and damage the thread, you will have to get it tapped out by a professional bike mechanic. It is also worth getting the threads tapped out after a respray, in case the new paint has choked the threads. Remember to lightly coat the thread of the bolt with anti-seize grease.

A similar method of fixing is shown on page 49. Here, a small extension plate is bolted onto the gear hanger and the derailleur itself is fitted to the rear end of the extension. This places the derailleur further back than usual, which allows much larger sprockets to be fitted. Fitting the rear derailleur this way is particularly suitable for quality hybrid bikes and similar. To remove the rear derailleur, undo the socket-headed bolt in the same way as the pivot bolt.

The final way of installing the rear derailleur on the frame is shown on page 51. This method is used on budget bikes, which do not have a built-in gear hanger. Instead, a separate bracket is bolted to the rear end, with a specially-shaped oval nut on the inside. To remove the derailleur, you have to remove the back wheel first, then remove the bottom jockey wheel or break the chain. Finally, you loosen the fixing screw at the back of the bracket and pull the derailleur forward, away from the frame. When re-installing, you will find the inside face of the special nut is shaped to fit into the wheel slot in the rear end. As you tighten the bolt, stop the nut turning by holding it with a wrench on the flats. Do not overtighten because the bracket is held in place by the wheel as well.

1 This shows the way to remove a rear derailleur by breaking the chain. Hold the derailleur with one hand while you undo the pivot bolt with a long hex key.

2 If you are re-installing the derailleur later, take the opportunity to do a quick strip down and clean (see page 54). Lubricate the jockey wheels with waterproof grease.

5 Turn the pedals slowly and push the bottom part of your rear derailleur away from you with your thumb. Adjust the L screw if the chain does not jump onto the largest sprocket.

6 Fit the gear cable now, tensioning the inner before you do up the cable clamp. Snip any spare inner cable off close to the clamp and fit a cable end to prevent fraying.

Fine tuning index gears

1 If the indexing is having an off-day, increase or decrease the cable tension by turning the cable adjuster a quarter-turn. Experiment to find out which way is best.

2 Racing bikes with STI and Ergopower combined gear shifters usually have a thumb adjuster on the down tube so you can alter cable tension when riding along.

3 When fitting the rear derailleur to the frame, it is easier to screw the top pivot bolt into the gear hanger if you steady it by tucking your forefinger behind the gear hanger.

4 You can fit the chain now. Then start adjusting the throw of the rear derailleur by turning the H screw until the jockey wheels align with the outer edge of the top sprocket.

7 Check that the outer cable is arranged in smooth, large radius curves. Then go through the final adjustment procedure on pages 50 to 53 and give the bike a road test.

DAMAGED GEAR HANGERS

Hanging off the side of the frame, the rear derailleur and gear hanger often gets damaged when a bike falls over. To prevent this from happening, replace the standard top pivot bolt with a breakaway bolt. This provides a weak link that snaps off to stop the derailleur from getting damaged. For an easy way to straighten the hanger on a steel frame, see page 27. Other materials are less forgiving, so frames are often fitted with a replaceable gear hanger, retained by a short-socket head bolt. However, each frame needs a different hanger, so buy a spare when you buy your new frame.

CHAIN CLASHES

There is a third adjuster screw on most rear derailleurs which you do not normally touch. But if you fit a new cluster or rear derailleur and the top jockey wheel touches the top or bottom sprocket, turn the angle adjuster screw until the jockey wheel just misses the sprocket. For SRAM gears, see page 52.

BOTTOM BRACKET FRONT DERAILLEUR

To save assembly time, some bike manufacturers now fit the front derailleur on a bracket that is held in place by the sealed bottom bracket cartridge. This is not a problem, apart from the fact that you cannot adjust the position of the front derailleur at all. If you ever want to install a larger or smaller chainring, consider replacing this type with a conventional band-on front derailleur.

WHEN YOU NEED TO DO THIS JOB:
◆ The old rear derailleur is worn out.
◆ A rear derailleur has been stripped down completely.

TIME:
◆ 30 minutes to install a new rear derailleur, plus another 30 minutes to adjust and test gear change.

DIFFICULTY 𝄢
◆ Care is needed when screwing the pivot bolt into the gear hanger. Otherwise easier than overhauling a rear derailleur.

SPECIAL TOOLS
◆ None.

Front derailleur: care and adjustment

Front derailleurs are not temperamental like rear derailleurs— once set up, they go for ages before needing attention.

Front derailleurs all work on the same principle but there are detailed variations that are very significant. Most recent MTBs have a front derailleur indexed like a rear derailleur, with a 1-2-3 indicator on the shifter. Older MTBs usually have a front derailleur that works with a friction gear lever.

The newest type of MTB front derailleur has a cable that pulls from the top. This allows the cable to be routed along the top tube, avoiding the filth and mud thrown up from the road. But you can still buy bottom-pull front derailleurs for MTBs, as well as some designs that adapt to either top or bottom-pull.

All road bikes are fitted with bottom pull front derailleurs, including the ones specially designed for the narrow chains used with 9- and 10-speed rear derailleurs.

The shape and size of the chain cage varies more than any other part. The triple drivetrain fitted to MTBs usually have a big jump between the smallest and largest chainring, so mountain bike front derailleurs have a deep, heavily stepped chain cage.

The double chainrings on most road bikes have a smaller jump between them. So smaller and lighter chain cages can be used, although triple drivetrain and matching front derailleurs are now available for road bikes as well. Do not try to make an MTB front derailleur work on a road bike or vice versa.

A front derailleur with a clip that fits round the frame is known as a band-on front derailleur. When buying, check that the clip is the correct diameter for the down tube on your bike. However, shims are sometimes supplied to allow for different diameters.

FRONT DERAILLEUR ADJUSTER SCREWS

Sometimes the adjuster screws on front derailleurs are marked H = High = the biggest chainring, and L = Low = the smallest chainring. This is similar to a rear derailleur, but the letters are often so small that on the front derailleur it is very hard to read them. To identify which screw is which, just give the outer one an experimental half-turn.

1 When fitting a new front derailleur or tuning up an old one, position the outer plate of the chain cage between 1 and 3 mm above the teeth of the outer chainring. The red tab on a new derailleur is to help you get this right.

2 Arrange the outer plate of the chain cage exactly in line with the chainrings, then tighten the clamp around the seat tube. The chain should be fitted at this point but has been left out here to make it easier to see what is going on.

3 Fit the chain onto the inner chainring and adjust the L screw of the front derailleur so that the inner plate of the chain cage is about 0.5 mm clear of the chain. Spin the cranks to check that the chain does not touch the chain cage.

4 Next, lift the chain up onto the big chainring and operate the front changer with your fingers. Adjust the H screw of the front derailleur so that the outer plate of the chain cage is also 0.5 mm clear of the chain, which is close.

5 Fit the cable at this point, checking that the inner cable moves freely and that the outer is not kinked. Make sure also that it is slotted correctly into the cable stops. Lube the inner cable and the derailleur.

6 Feed the inner cable between the chain stays and tension it with one hand and tighten the cable clamp with the other. Now check that the front derailleur changes from ring to ring without delay.

7 On an indexed derailleur, check that the change from the inner to the middle chainring works particularly well. If it does not, increase cable tension with the cable adjuster until you get an instant change with one click of the shifter. You may also have to make very fine adjustments to the H and L screws to reduce noise or improve the gear change. Finally, cut off surplus cable.

Fitting a front derailleur

1 To remove a front derailleur, remove the inner and outer cable. Then take out the clamp bolt and pull the derailleur back, away from the frame.

2 Undo the nut and bolt at the back of the chain cage and pull the plates apart. Slip the front derailleur off the chain. Reverse steps to install a new one.

WHEN YOU NEED TO DO THIS JOB
◆ If the chain jumps off when you are changing from one chainring to another.

TIME
◆ 10 minutes to adjust or remove the front derailleur.
◆ Another 10 minutes to check adjustment with a test ride.

DIFFICULTY
◆ Quite easy.

Gear shifters

Friction gear levers are easy to strip down. But index shifters have many tiny parts and should only be opened up when absolutely necessary. Rotary handlebar shifters must never be taken apart.

Nearly all mountain bikes are fitted with index gears controlled by shifters mounted on the handlebars. Only a few mountain bikes have friction levers and they usually just control the front derailleur, not the rear one.

Index shifters work either on a ratchet principle or a stroke principle. You can tell if it is a ratchet lever because there is a sharp click that you can feel and hear when you move the gear lever. Inside this type of lever is a round plate with a series of holes which represent each gear position. A spring-loaded ball bearing engages with the holes in the plate and creates the definite positions that you can feel as you use the lever. You should only take this type of lever apart if you can no longer feel the definite positions, or if it seems to have seized up and will not respond to a long soak in silicon lube or similar.

Stroke shifters are even more complicated. Although you can sometimes undo the central screw, remove the cover and then clean, lubricate with light grease, and fit new cables, you should never attempt to go any further. Where indicators are fitted, you usually have to remove two small screws to take off the indicator unit, then undo the central socket-head screw, which enables you to separate the shifter from the brake lever.

STI and Ergopower road bike levers also work on the stroke principle and should only be taken apart by experienced mechanics. However, many road bikes have friction down-tube levers—the rest have indexed levers that work on the ratchet principle.

Friction levers can be stripped down without difficulty, but they are rarely problematic—it is only necessary if they have been soaked in lube and you cannot tighten the center screw enough to make them hold their adjustment.

1 Basic thumbshifter levers are found on budget mountain bikes. The large button at the front allows you to select friction gears if the indexing breaks down when you are out. They fit with a simple clamp.

2 Like most handlebar shifters, maintenance consists of an occasional spray with aerosol lube, then a wipe over. Try to direct the spray at the cable nipple, then operate the gear lever a few times.

3 Rapidfire Plus levers have a separate lever for up and down shifts. They must never be stripped down. To lube, remove the rubber cap over the nipple, if fitted, and squirt aerosol into the nipple recess.

4 If you find it awkward to use any type of shifter, try altering its position on the handlebar. Loosen off the clamp bolt and move the assembly to a more comfortable position.

5 Quality road bikes usually have two down tube levers. The front derailleur lever is sometimes friction while the rear derailleur usually has an indexed lever. You can usually select index or friction by turning the central screw.

6 The cable fits into the lever on down-tube levers, so do not direct the lube there. Instead, aim the aerosol at the outside of the central housing, where it is more likely to find its way into the ratchet mechanism where it is needed.

INDEX SHIFTER

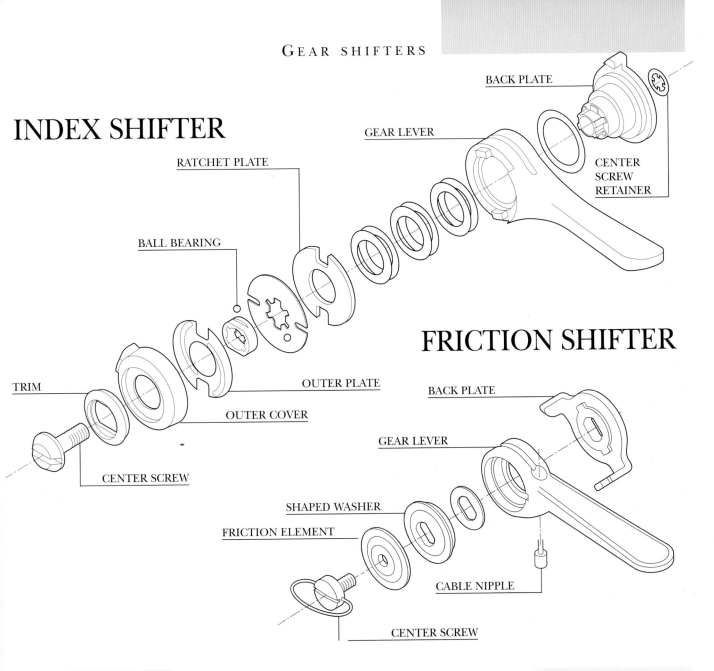

BACK PLATE

GEAR LEVER

CENTER SCREW RETAINER

RATCHET PLATE

BALL BEARING

TRIM

OUTER PLATE

OUTER COVER

CENTER SCREW

FRICTION SHIFTER

BACK PLATE

GEAR LEVER

SHAPED WASHER

FRICTION ELEMENT

CABLE NIPPLE

CENTER SCREW

7 Most down-tube shifters screw into bosses fixed to the frame, though a few have a band-on fixing. To remove, undo the central screw and pull off. To refit, make sure you locate the square cut-out on the back plate correctly.

TIME
◆ 1 minute to lube.
◆ 1 hour to strip and re-assemble down-tube ratchet lever.

DIFFICULTY
◆ Lube is easy but stripping ratchet levers is not, so only tackle this job if you have to. Most handlebar and rotary shifters are too complicated for anybody except the manufacturers to cope with.

Fitting new gear cables

When they become frayed or sticky with congealed oil, gear cables must be changed. Unfortunately there is a vast variety of different gear shifters, so read the pages covering gear shifters first, then go through steps 1 to 5 until you find the design nearest to yours.

All inner cables look very similar but that can be misleading. So when buying, specify whether you have indexed gears or not. The high quality cables for indexed gears are stiffer than normal ones and both cables and housing are often specially treated to reduce friction. That means it is okay to use indexed cables on ordinary gears, but not the other way round. If you use non-indexed cables on indexed gears, it will affect the gear change and you will have to adjust them more often.

The next problem is that Shimano uses one type of nipple, while Campagnolo and Suntour use a slightly different one. So you also have to specify the make of gear, but even then, you sometimes have to file the nipple a little until it fits snugly into the shifter.

When fitting new inner cables, check the housing for kinks and breaks as well. On indexed gears, it is best to use ready-made housing with metal ferrules rather than making complete cables up yourself. Anyway, special outer cable is made for indexed gears. This has separate wires running the length of the cable, held together by a plastic cover. This kind of outer cable does not compress when the inner is fully tensioned, so it does not affect the way the indexing works.

Many cable clamps are designed so that the inner cable wraps around the clamp bolt slightly. There may be a curved slot to install the cable into, but you should make a mental note of the old cable path before removing the old inner cable, just in case.

Lubricate inner and outer cables with silicon, mineral oil, and synthetic lubricants only, not grease.

CABLE SEALS

The length of outer cable between the frame and the rear derailleur can get filled with dirt and water and this has a major effect on the performance of the rear derailleur. Fit a new outer cable every time you fit a new inner and fit a cable seal as well to prevent the gear change deteriorating again.

MTB and hybrid

1 Some handlebar shifters have a partly hidden cable recess. Look for it by moving the lever forward, then tracing the path of the cable around the lever. If you screw the cable adjuster right in, the nipple may pop out of the recess.

2 On underbar set-ups, the inner cable fits into the shifter between the top of the gear levers and the handlebar. Gently pry out the rubber cap covering the nipple recess, where fitted. Select top gear and push nipple out of recess.

Run the outer cable from the frame to the rear derailleur in a smooth curve. Carefully feed the inner through the cable adjuster and clamp, then seat the outer in the cable adjuster.

3 Access to the inner gear cable is concealed by a screw-in plug on many designs including rotary shifters. Unscrew the plug and pull out the old cable first.

4 When fitting the inner cable, you may find it easier to work from underneath, as here. Hold the cable between finger and thumb and gradually feed it into the changer.

5 When the end of the cable emerges from the cable adjuster, feed the end into the outer cable and keep pushing it through until it pops out the other end. Then pull it tight, carefully seating the end of the outer in the cable adjuster.

6 This method of feeding the cable through the cable entry, through the changer, and into the outer cable works well on many designs. You must lube the inner cable as it enters the outer but take care not to kink either of the cables.

Sports bike gear cables

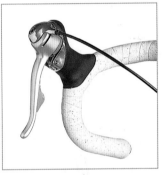

1 Disconnect the derailleur end of the inner cable and pull it away through the outer. Then push the gear lever forward and hold it while you push the nipple up and out of the recess. Grip the cable with pliers if your fingers slip.

2 With down-tube shifters, the cables usually pass under the bike and through plastic guides on the bottom bracket shell. Check that the guides are not damaged or blocked, then carefully uncoil the new cable to prevent any kinks.

3 Make sure that the gear lever is in top and that the chain is on the top sprocket. Feed the inner cable through the cable adjuster, pull tight, and do up the cable clamp. Finally, cut off any spare cable and fit a cable end.

4 On STI levers, the nipple fits in the outer side of the brake levers and can only be seen when the brakes are applied. On Ergopower and Sachs levers, you have to peel the rubber hood back before you can see the nipple.

WHEN YOU NEED TO DO THIS JOB
◆ If the cables are frayed or sticky, leading to a heavy gear change.
◆ When there is a mystery fault with the indexing and lube does not help.

TIME
◆ 30 minutes to install a rear derailleur cable, less to install a front derailleur cable.

DIFFICULTY
◆ Easy to install new cables on a racing bike with down-tube shifters, but handlebar and twist grip shifters are very tough at times.

TOOLS
◆ A cable cutter is desirable.

READY-MADE CABLES
Once the cable from the frame to the rear derailleur has started to deteriorate, there is no point trying to clean it out again with thin wire or aerosol lube. Replace with a short length of outer cable made for this job and sold individually. No need to buy a complete cable set.

Sturmey Archer and Torpedo hub gears

Too many utility bike riders struggle along because their hub gears do not work. Yet they are the easiest gears of all to adjust and work really well in city traffic.

Inside all hub gears are a lot of carefully machined parts that have more in common with the automatic gearbox on a car than with anything on a bike. Fortunately these internal parts seldom go wrong and on the rare occasions when there is a fault, it is probably due to wear and a complete new unit is usually the answer. You should never try to strip down a hub gear by yourself, as it is unlikely that you will ever get it back together again correctly without special tools and know-how.

The commonest problem on a Sturmey is finding that you can only pedal in one gear – somehow you are in neutral when the gear lever is in other positions. The other big fault is slipping in the gears – there is a coughing noise, the pedals jerk round suddenly and then go back to normal. This happens more often going uphill. These and most other faults are more often caused by incorrect adjustment of the cable, a broken cable or a broken control chain than anything else.

Follow the basic process given in steps 1 to 3 to install new cables or control chains and to keep the gears in adjustment. New cables come complete with inner and outer and on older bikes, the outer is positioned with an adjustable heavy-duty frame clamp. If you ever find that you cannot adjust the cable correctly, adjust the position of the frame clamp. If the cable runs over a pulley, check that it turns freely.

The latest Sturmey Archers are sealed and do not need oiling. But if there is a black plastic oil port on the hub body, feed a few drops of light oil into the hub every couple of weeks.

Wheel bearings are cup and cone type, adjusted in the usual way, but you will probably need a special wrench. Adjust on the opposite side from the chain.

See page 66 for more details of Torpedo three speed gears.

Remove back wheel

1 On hub gear bikes, the gear cable connects with the back axle, so the first step is to separate them. Undo the knurled wheel on the gear cable one quarter-turn, then undo the adjuster about twelve turns to release the cable.

2 Slacken both wheel nuts with a wrench, then undo them the rest of the way with your fingers. To prevent the axle turning, special washers fit around the axle and into the frame. Place the wheel nuts and washers to one side.

New cable and adjustment

1 Check first that the control chain moves freely and is screwed right into the axle. Undo it one half-turn (at the most) to align it with the control cable. If the chain is stiff or broken, simply unscrew the old one and screw in a new one.

2 Put the gear lever into low and pry out the nipple of the old inner cable, then unscrew the outer from the back of the lever. Fit the new cable, clamp the cable at the correct length, and tighten the adjuster up to knurled nut.

WHEN YOU NEED TO DO THIS JOB
◆ Cable is broken.
◆ Control chain is stiff or broken.
◆ Gears will not engage. Or they slip (step 3).

TIME
◆ 15 minutes to install new cable.
◆ 2 minutes for step 3.

DIFFICULTY
◆ It is easy to install a new cable, but adjusting the gears can be awkward.

TOOLS
Special cone wrench.

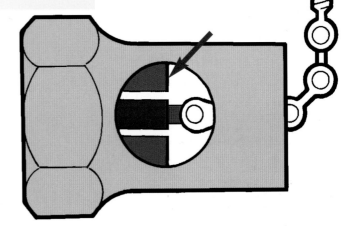

3 Push the axle forward with your thumbs, but try to hold the wheel as it drops away to keep it from bouncing around. Now support the frame with one hand while you lift the chain off the sprocket and put the wheel to one side.

4 When re-installing, replace the shaped axle washers. Then do up the wheel nuts lightly, pulling the wheel back so that it is centralized, with about 12mm of play in the chain. Tighten the wheel nuts, giving each side a turn at a time.

Looking down through the inspection hole, the arrow indicates where the shoulder of the control rod should be aligned with the end of the axle.

Torpedo hub gears

3 Select N or 2 on the gear lever and look through the inspection hole in the axle nut. Clean out if necessary. Screw the adjuster up or down until the shoulder is exactly in line with the end of the axle (see the diagram on this page).

1 Check that the control chain flexes easily and that it is screwed fully home into the axle. Also make sure that the cable is undamaged and is not frayed where it goes over the pulley. Select H or 3 position on the gear lever.

2 The Torpedo cable comes in one piece, with a plastic ratchet that clicks onto the control chain. The length of the inner cable is adjusted with a hex key via the cable clamp, so that the ratchet just reaches the control chain.

3 Bring the end of the control chain and the ratchet together, then push the ratchet onto the control chain as far as you can using minimum force. Check that the cable feels fairly taut, but not under any tension.

Nexus and Sachs hub gears

Torpedo hub gears are similar to Sturmey Archer but the new generation of multi-speed hubs opens up a new era for city bikes.

Torpedo hub gears (see previous page) are very straightforward three-speed units. Unlike a Sturmey Archer, they will always give you drive—you may not get the gear you want, but at least you can always get one. The main thing that can go wrong is the cable. It will either need tightening up or you will have to install a new one. Use steps 1 to 3 to help you with both these jobs. If you need to remove the back wheel, disconnect the gear cable as in step 4, then use the same procedure as when removing a Sturmey wheel.

Shimano Nexus gears have either four or seven speeds. The seven-speed version has a very wide range of gears, right down to a crawler gear for steep hills.

The main problem with Nexus is the cable going out of adjustment, which is indicated by unusual noises or inability to select a gear. If a hub brake is fitted and there is an unusual noise when using the brakes, or the brakes are very sharp, there is not enough grease in the brake.

Either get it topped up by your local bike shop or fill the brake body with brake grease through the topping-up hole on the outside of the brake unit. You have to get the gear refilled with grease and serviced every six months anyway.

When removing a wheel with a Nexus hub, select first gear. Then disconnect the cable and the brake arm, if fitted.

Most of these hub gears are sealed and do not need lubricating, but check with the supplying dealer if you are not sure.

Fitting a new cable and

1 When fitting a new cable or adjusting the gears, select fourth gear on the gear shifter using the rotary hand grip before doing anything else. The figure '4' must appear in the round indicator window.

2 To remove the old gear cable, undo the three tiny Phillips screws holding the cover onto the gear shifter. The screw heads fit from underneath, so be careful not to let them drop on the floor.

5 Thread the new inner cable around the three rollers in the gear shifter and feed the end through the cable adjuster and the outer cable. Push the slack through and seat the nipple carefully.

6 Push the inner cable down through the outer and the cassette. When it emerges inside the rear drop out, lead the cable around the pulley and through the cable clamp. Pull the inner cable tight.

7 Tighten the cable clamp grub screw to keep the cable under tension. Then screw the cable adjusting bolt at the end of the outer cable in or out until the two red lines line up. Road test the bike to check that the gear changes go through easily and that the gear is silent, apart from when changing gear or a second or so afterwards.

Adjusting Nexus gears

3 Working from the top, lift off the silver cover. That allows you to pry the cable nipple out with a screwdriver. Cut the inner cable at a convenient point and pull it all out of the outer cable.

4 That leaves the rest of the cable clamped to the hub. Undo the socket head grub screw and pull out the remaining part of the old inner cable. To install the new cable, start at the shifter end.

WHEN YOU NEED TO DO THIS JOB
◆ Control chain has broken or gone stiff.
◆ Cable has frayed or broken.
◆ You can't find all the gears.

TIME
◆ 10 minutes to install new cable on either Torpedo or Sachs 7-speed.
◆ 5 minutes to adjust Torpedo cable.
◆ 2 minutes to check click box location.

DIFFICULTY
◆ Very easy—much easier than adjusting Sturmey Archer.

Sachs 7-speed hub gears

1 If you suspect that the cable or lever on a seven-speed Sachs hub gear has been damaged, it can only be replaced as a complete unit. So undo the lever clamp, pull off the handlebars and undo all the cable fastenings.

2 There is no need to adjust the cable, as it is sealed into the click box. This fits onto the end of the axle. Check by loosening the mounting screw occasionally and pushing the click box onto the axle, retightening the screw by hand.

3 Sitting on the end of the axle, a click box is quite vulnerable to damage when a bike falls over. Park your bike carefully to prevent this from happening and always fit the guard when you refit the back wheel, just in case.

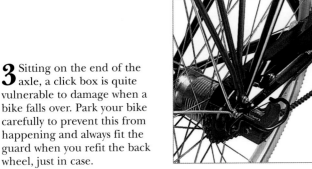

CHAPTER 5

CHAIN, PEDALS, & CRANKS

The crankset converts the muscle power of your legs into mechanical energy, which is then transmitted to the wheels. It is this nearly direct conversion of human energy into mechanical power that makes a bicycle so efficient.

drivetrains: components

Take a moment to identify the type of crankset and bottom bracket you are dealing with. Cranks are usually cotterless but there are also cottered and one piece designs. Bottom brackets can be the sealed or the adjustable type on newer bikes but you are more likely to come across the adjustable variety on older ones.

CRANK
BOLT

SPIDER

CHAINRING

CHAINRING
BOLT

CRANK

This crankset from the LX group is cotterless and can be removed by undoing the crank bolts counter-clockwise with a long hex key. Chainrings vary in size, according to the gearing you want. But they also vary in the number of chainring bolts, usually four or five, and pitch circle diameter (PCD). This is the diameter of the circle joining all the crank bolts.

PEDAL

1 This crankset is a modern cotterless one, identified by the socket-headed crank bolt. Older types of cotterless have standard hexagon crank bolts, often fitted with a slotted dust cap as well.

2 Standard bottom brackets have an axle supported by ball bearings that run in one bearing cup each side. Frequent stripping and greasing can be needed. They are usually fitted with a toothed lockring.

3 Some standard bottom brackets have a six-sided lockring and adjustable bearing cup requiring a large wrench. Others have two neat pairs of holes in the adjustable cup, to allow for a pin spanner.

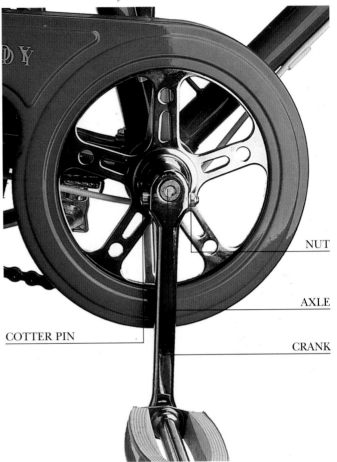

NUT

AXLE

CRANK

COTTER PIN

4 You can identify a cottered crankset by the cotters that run across the top of the cranks, locking them to the axle. This type of crankset is found on elderly and budget bikes only and they are nearly always made of chromed steel. Cottered cranksets are fitted to a standard adjustable bottom bracket.

5 Wear trainers or some other type of lightweight shoe with standard pedals and toe clips. On budget bikes and kids' bikes, the pedals can be made of plastic and cannot be stripped down or adjusted, so consider an upgrade.

6 There are many designs of clipless pedals around and prices are now low enough for them to be a serious option for many riders. They are more comfortable for long journeys and transmit muscle power to the crankset more efficiently.

7 When buying, get advice from a reliable bike shop or an expert rider. Take care that the shoes are a good fit and are also comfortable. BMX pedals (above) are double-sided for easy use in the heat of the moment.

DOUBLE-SIDED PEDALS

A popular type of MTB pedal is fitted with a clipless mechanism on one side and a platform on the other. Useful in difficult terrain when you are on and off the bike.

Drivetrain: care and inspection

As the miles go by, wear gradually builds up in the drivetrain. To maintain maximum efficiency, check it over every few months.

It is the build-up of gritty deposits on the chain, sprockets, and chainring that causes the most wear in the drivetrain. Keep the chain clean and well lubricated, and you will slow down wear by preventing this build-up.

If the drivetrain is neglected, the gritty deposit acts as an abrasive paste, so every time the chain rubs against the teeth of the chainring or sprockets, a tiny fragment of metal is worn away. Multiply that by the number of times the chain slips on and off the teeth of the chainring in 1,000 miles and the amount of wear soon becomes significant.

Chainrings are usually made of an aluminum alloy. The cheaper types are quite soft but luckily they pick up a hard layer on the surface as they are used and this slows down the wear. The more expensive chainrings are made of harder alloys or are anodized to combat wear. Either way, the steel chain and sprockets usually wear faster than the alloy chainring.

Once a new drivetrain has done a thousand miles or so, the sprockets and chain are worn into each other. If you then try to run a chain on different sprockets, it may not mesh properly. You may get away with it but there will probably be a regular cough or jerk as you turn the cranks, particularly when putting on the pressure. The only way out of this is to replace the sprockets and chain, but do not wait too long or the worn chain will accelerate the wear on the chainring as well.

1 Chain rings are fixed to the spider of the crankset with four or five fixing bolts. So the first part of the inspection is to check they are tight. The sleeve nut at the back of the chainring may turn as you do so—stop it turning with a screwdriver.

2 If the cranks are loose on the axle, they sometimes creak as you ride along. But do not rely on this. Test for movement by holding one crank while you wiggle the other. If you feel it moving, tighten the crank bolts immediately.

3 The next check is for wear or play in the bottom bracket bearing. Hold each crank near the pedal and try to move them diagonally. If both cranks move the same amount, the bottom bracket needs changing or adjusting.

4 Lift the chain right off the chainring. Then, using the frame as a fixed point, turn the crank and see if the distance between the chainring and the frame varies. If it does, take off the chainring so you can see if the spider is bent as well.

LOOSE CRANKS
If the left-hand crank is worn and you cannot tighten it enough to stop it moving, try filing or grinding some metal off the reverse side of the square hole, where it fits on the axle. Assemble with Loctite and tighten as hard as you can.

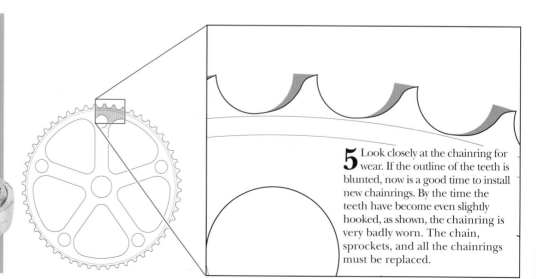

5 Look closely at the chainring for wear. If the outline of the teeth is blunted, now is a good time to install new chainrings. By the time the teeth have become even slightly hooked, as shown, the chainring is very badly worn. The chain, sprockets, and all the chainrings must be replaced.

CHAINLINE AND GEAR SELECTION

For minimum wear, a chain should run as straight as possible. But since derailleur gears work by making the chain run out of line, the bike should be set up so that a line through the middle of the chainrings hits the middle of the sprocket cluster. Check the chainline by eye and if it seems to be out, ask a professional mechanic to check the length of the bottom bracket axle, the rear hub packing, and the alignment of the frame.

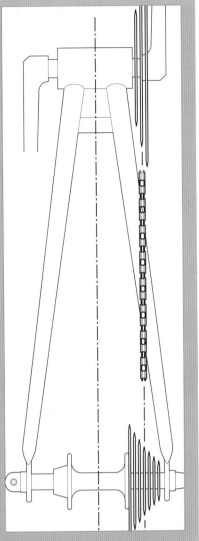

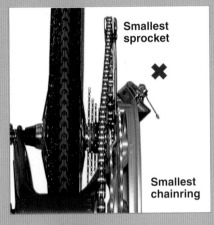

Smallest sprocket

✖

Smallest chainring

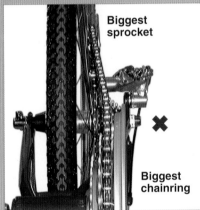

Biggest sprocket

✖

Biggest chainring

Avoid selecting gears where the chain has to bend almost in a curve as the chain will wear very fast, as shown on the left. Using these gears, you will also waste a lot of energy because of the extra friction created. If you ever have to use them, change gear again as soon as you can.

Perfect chainline on a bike with 21 speeds—seven sprockets and three chainrings.

WHEN YOU NEED TO DO THIS JOB

◆ Every few months on a bike in regular use.
◆ When you are overhauling a neglected bike to bring it back into regular use.
◆ To assess how much you will have to do to bring a second-hand bike up to scratch.

TIME

◆ 15 minutes for a complete inspection, to include checking chain wear and chainline.

DIFFICULTY 𝓨𝓨𝓨

◆ The hardest part is working out exactly which one of the various possible problems with the cranks is causing the problem.
◆ It's also quite difficult to check the chainline with absolute accuracy, which is desirable on bikes with 14 speeds or more.

TOOLS

◆ Clearly marked steel ruler.
◆ Meter steel ruler helps in checking chainline.

Chain: clean and lube

A clean chain in good condition transmits 95 percent of the power you produce to the rear wheel. That is much better than any other transmission system can do.

Nearly all modern bikes have a $^3/_{32}$ in chain. The only exceptions you are likely to come across are basic kids' bikes, bikes with hub gears, and track bikes. These usually have $^1/_8$in chains which are slightly wider and heavier. The width of the teeth on the chainring and sprockets match the width of the chain, so you cannot mix and match these components.

If you are buying parts for a bike that could have an $^1/_8$ in chain, look for the spring link (see page 77) or compare it with the chain on a bike with gears. If this confirms the bike has a $^1/_8$ in chain, tell the retailer so he knows what size components you need.

All bikes with derailleur gears have a $^3/_{32}$ in chain, even kids' models. When you want to break a $^3/_{32}$ in chain and join it back together, you sometimes have to use a special chain tool. But increasing numbers of chains are fitted with Power Links or similar designs, which have a patented joining link (see the Blue Box on page 78). The only way to shorten either size of chain when installing a new one is with a proper chain tool.

Basic $^3/_{32}$ in chains are most suitable for use with five sprocket clusters. More expensive $^3/_{32}$ in chains are usually narrower and more flexible, so they work better on six- and seven-sprocket clusters. Bikes with seven- and eight- sprocket clusters should only be fitted with very flexible, high-quality chains, as they have to run a long way out of line. Nine-speed drivetrains use a narrower, more expensive, but even more flexible chain. The latest ten sprocket clusters only work with their own special chain.

Automatic chain cleaner

1 Fill the chain cleaner with solvent up to the mark. Hook the support behind the rear derailleur and then close the lid. The chain must pass through the middle of the brushes.

2 Slowly turn the pedals backwards so that the brushes revolve, scrubbing the crud off the chain. Repeat with clean solvent if necessary. Do not throw solvent away – recycle it.

3 There are several different designs of chain cleaner around, although each type is sold under several different brand names. All are made of plastic, so be very gentle with them. When the solvent has done its work, pour it into a lidded jam jar and let the dirt settle out, ready for re-use next time.

SPECIAL CLEANING FLUIDS

Chain cleaning machines are often sold with a bottle of cleaning fluid as a special offer. But once that bottle is finished, a standard degreaser will work fine in the machine and probably cost a lot less. However, you must dispose of these solvents in the dustbin, preferably pouring them onto a wad of newspaper so that they are absorbed. Do not ever pour them down a sink or road drain where they may leak into the ground water and contaminate the environment. You could use a more environmentally-friendly alternative but the residue still has to be disposed of carefully because it is contaminated with the hydrocarbons used in chain lubricants.

Easy chain cleaning

1 If your chain is caked in mud, hose it clean first. But if it is just covered in oily dirt, remove the worst of the crud with a cloth. Take care to clean the back of the chain as well.

2 If the chain is dirty, the sprockets and chainring will be too. So use the edge of a cloth to get between the sprockets and then wipe the teeth of the chainrings as well.

3 The cloth will not reach between the chain rollers, so spray with solvent and scrub with an old toothbrush next. Then flush away with an old sponge and plenty of water.

4 When the chain is clean, lubricate first with a heavy oil. Let that soak into the rivets and then spray with an aerosol lube. Direct the lube at the sprockets so they get some too.

Checking chain wear

1 As chains wear, they also stretch. So as a basic check, try lifting one rivet only at the front of the chainring. If that opens up a big gap between the chain and the chainring, the chain is worn.

2 Measuring the length of a known number of chain links is a more reliable method of gauging wear. Use a steel ruler because they are easy to read, then position the zero of the ruler on the center of a rivet.

3 Count out twelve links of chain. If the chain is new, the twelve links will measure 12in to the center of the rivet. A badly worn chain, one that is ready for the dustbin right away, will measure 12$^{1}/_{8}$in.

What Chain?

If you don't know which type of chain you have, clean the side plates and check the brand name. Sedis, Sachs, and Taya are the most common brands of standard chain. The rivets can be pushed out and back in again with any chain tool.

Shimano chains are marked UG, HG or IG and the rivet heads are slightly larger than the hole. When they are pushed out, the rivet holes become enlarged. That means special black joining rivets must be used to join the chain up again.

WHEN YOU NEED TO DO THIS JOB
◆ Every month when the bike is in daily use.
◆ When the chain is visibly dirty.
◆ After a ride through mud or heavy rain.

TIME
◆ 15 minutes to clean a dirty chain; another 15 minutes to clean your hands. Consider using disposable latex gloves, obtainable from almost any local drug store.

DIFFICULTY
◆ No special problems.

TOOLS
◆ Auto chain cleaner, old toothbrush, lots of cloths, newspaper or old carpet to absorb any drips.

Chain: remove and replace

Sometimes you simply have to split the chain, but every time you do so, you increase the chances of the chain breaking.

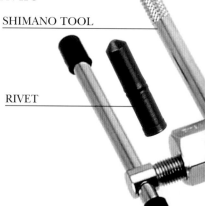

SHIMANO TOOL

RIVET

When you are faced with a really dirty or rusty chain, it is usually best to install a new one. But if you want to bring an old chain back into use, try soaking it in paraffin or diesel oil, until it is as clean and flexible as new. This involves taking the chain off the bike, so the first thing is to identify which type of chain you are dealing with (see page 75). Once you know that, you can pick the correct method of removal and re-installation.

If you find you are dealing with a Shimano chain, you will need a replacement pin to rejoin the chain. You cannot use the old one. There might be a spare one concealed in the chain tool but if not, you will have to get a new pin from a bike shop before you can do this job. These replacement rivets are black and have a long stalk that has to be broken off with pliers. Do not ever remove one of these black rivets after it has been used to join a chain. If you have to split the chain again, push out a silver-headed rivet instead.

Standard chain

1 Wind the punch out and position the chain on the guides furthest from the punch. Shimano chain tools work fine on standard chains—you just have to adjust the support screw so that it presses on the back of the chain.

WHEN YOU NEED TO DO THIS JOB
◆ The chain is badly worn.
◆ The chain is rusty.
◆ You cannot undo the jockey wheel bolts.

TIME
◆ Allow 20 minutes the first time you split the chain as you will need to take your time and check each stage carefully.

DIFFICULTY ✗✗✗✗
◆ You will have to use quite a lot of force to push out the rivet, which makes this job a bit nerve wracking until you're used to it. Also, when working on a Shimano chain, you must be very careful to press out a normal silver-headed rivet, and never a black-headed joining rivet.

TOOLS
◆ Standard or Shimano chain tool.
◆ Hefty pliers and small file.

Shimano HG and IG chain

1 Select a silver rivet—never a black-headed one—to push out. Fit the chain onto the guides furthest from the punch and adjust the support screw so that it firmly supports the back of the chain plate.

2 Check the punch is centered, and then start pushing the rivet out. You will probably be surprised at how much force is needed. Drive the rivet right out, undo the chain tool, and separate the two links.

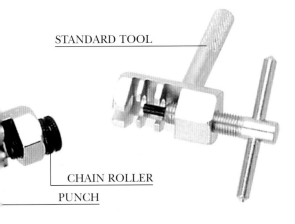

STANDARD TOOL

CHAIN ROLLER

PUNCH

2 Make sure the chain is seated securely on the guides. Next, wind the punch in until the pointed end hits the dimple in the center of the rivet. Check that the punch is exactly centered, then screw it in just under six full turns. It will be stiff at first, but should become easier after the first half turn.

3 With the rivet out but not all the way out, flex the chain to separate it. If it does not come apart, push the rivet out a bit further but not right out. Try to leave a short length of rivet inside the chain plate, so you can snap the links together when joining the chain up again.

3 To re-install the chain, push the new rivet into both holes in the side plate so that the tip is just visible. Slot the chain into the chain tool, then screw in the punch until it hits the center of the new rivet.

4 Wind the new rivet in with a Shimano-type chain tool until the groove comes out of the other side of the rivet. Snap off the bit that sticks out. If it does not break cleanly, smooth the end with a file.

Prying open master link on ⅛in chain

1 Utility bikes fitted with ⅛in chains often have a chainguard to protect the chain from dirt. It is easier to take the chain off if you remove the chainguard first.

2 Turn the cranks until you spot the master link. Lift the tail of the spring clip off the head of the rivet with a screwdriver. Take care or it will fly across the garage as you do so.

3 With the spring clip out of the way, dislodge the loose side plate by flexing the chain. Then pull out the rivet part of the spring or master link as well.

4 Re-join the chain by reversing the process for taking it off. The closed end of the spring clip must point in the direction in which the chain moves.

STIFF LITTLE LINKS

If you hear a regular cough or feel a regular jump through the pedals, one of the chain links is probably stiff. You can sometimes loosen up a stiff link by flexing the chain backward and forward with your thumbs, either side of the rivet. But if the rivet sticks out too far on one side, fit the chain tool with the punch touching the rivet that sticks out. Then push the rivet in a tiny fraction by turning the handle about sixty degrees.

Installing a new chain

Installing a new chain is a bit more complicated than reusing an old one because you usually have to shorten it.

When you buy a new chain, there are extra links provided, just in case you use a very large chainring or sprocket, so you have to gauge the correct length.

This is important because the chain tensioning mechanism on a derailleur gear can only cope with a fixed amount of slack. It normally has to deal with the difference between the chain running on the big chainring and big sprocket, and the small chainring and the small sprocket. Unnecessary extra links of chain can cause the chain to jump off over rough ground and slowing down the gear change.

The best way to gauge chain length is to run the new chain through the rear derailleur, round the big chainring and the biggest sprocket, and then add two more links. But if you have an extra large range of gears, it is safer to add four extra links. Alternatively, select the biggest chainring and the smallest sprocket. Then set the chain length so that the chain cage points straight at the ground. On bikes with rear suspension, you must follow the maker's instructions.

On the other hand, if the existing chain seems to jump off a lot or the jockey arm on the rear derailleur goes right back in bottom gear, remove two links to see if that improves things.

Shimano transmissions are designed to be used with special HyperGlide (HG) or InterGlide (IG) chains. HG chains can be used with most Shimano transmission components, but IG chainrings and sprockets can only be used with IG chains and not with HG ones. However, Sachs and other makers now produce chains that work well with eight- and nine-speed HG and IG components as well as Campagnolo, Suntour, and Sachs ones. But do not forget that Campagnolo's ten-speed transmissions need special chains.

POWER CHAIN AND SIMILAR

Joining a chain with a chain tool is always a nuisance and creates a weak link. But Power Chains and similar designs eliminate the need for a chain tool, except when adjusting the length of a new chain. To join the chain, bring the ends together and press both pins of the connecting link through the rollers. The ends of the pins should sit slightly above the side plates. Then join the chain together by pulling hard on either side of the connecting link. The rivets should click into the narrow section of the side plate. To separate the chain, press the side plates together and force the inner links toward the connecting link.

Setting correct chain length

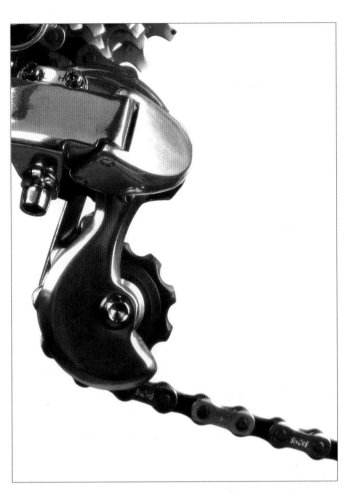

1 If you think there are too many links in a standard chain already on a bike, push one rivet out with a chain tool, leaving a short length in the sideplate.

2 Flex the chain sideways to separate the inner link from the outer. Then remove two links by pushing the next rivet all the way out.

3 No need to rivet the chain back together to check length. Just snap the inner link back into the outer, then replace on sprockets and chainring.

4 If the chain wraps round the biggest sprocket and chainring and rear derailleur without a strain, join the ends with a chain tool and then check that the link is not too stiff.

5 An alternative way of gauging chain length is to install the chain to the largest chain wheel and the smallest sprocket. Bring the ends together and overlap until the chain cage points at a right angle to the floor. Hold the rivet in your fingers to mark the correct chain length and remove the surplus with a chain tool.

BIKES WITH ONLY ONE SPROCKET
This category includes bikes with hub gears, single freewheels and fixed wheels. You can only adjust the chain tension on these by moving the back wheel. So when installing a new chain, position the wheel in the middle of the slot in the rear drop out. Then remove the spring link—see page 77—and wrap the chain around the chainring and sprocket. Pull the chain tight and grip the link where the ends overlap with two fingers. Remove the excess chain with a chain tool, join the ends with the spring link, and tension the chain so that there is about ½in of slack in the middle of the bottom run.

FIXED WHEEL
When riding a fixed wheel, you have to pedal all the time. This is an interesting change from gears, but remember that special track hubs are needed to prevent the sprocket from unscrewing.

Multiple Freewheels

Screw-on freewheels have 6, 7 or 8 sprockets but for 8, 9, and 10 speed transmissions, the cassette design is better.

Sprockets are the toothed cogs on the rear wheel that the chain runs on. When combined together, they are called a 'sprocket cluster' or 'cluster' for short. Multiple freewheels are also known as 'blocks' or 'cassettes'.

If you feel that the gear ratios are not right for you, fit different size sprockets but take expert advice before deciding which ratios to go for.

With screw-on freewheels, the sprockets screw onto the freewheel body which then screws onto the hub. You change the sprockets by holding the freewheel stationary with one chain whip and unscrewing the top sprockets with another chain whip.

In the cassette design, the freewheel mechanism is inside the cassette body, which is bolted to the hub. The sprockets fit into grooves on the outside.

HUB BEARING
LOCKNUT

Screw-on block

In the center of the block is a ring of cut outs. The dogs of the block remover fit into these cut outs so you can unscrew it from the hub. The sprocket teeth are shaped to speed up gear changes, with ramps on the side to guide the chain from sprocket to sprocket.

WHEN YOU NEED TO DO THIS JOB
◆ Sprocket teeth are worn.
◆ Freewheel is noisy and feels gritty.

TIME
◆ Allow 10 minutes to remove a screw-on freewheel. It's best to take your time.

DIFFICULTY ∤∤∤∤
◆ Take care – it is easy to damage the cut outs.

SPECIAL TOOLS
◆ Only attempt this job if you have the correct remover for the type of freewheel and it is completely undamaged.

Cassette freewheel

Freehubs are sealed and usually have a longer working life than a screw-on freewheel. They carry a 7-, 8-, 9- or 10-speed cassette, with heavily shaped sprocket teeth and large shifting ramps to improve the quality and speed of the gear change.

SPROCKET LOCKRING

REMOVING SINGLE SPROCKETS

To remove a single freewheel, position a blunt cold chisel in the recess in the center and hit it with a fairly heavy hammer. The freewheel unscrews in the normal, counterclockwise direction. Take care not to cut into the center of the freewheel with the cold chisel. On fixed wheel bikes, undo the lock ring in a clockwise direction, then unscrew the sprocket counterclockwise using a chain whip—see page 82.

Removing a screw-on freewheel

1 Undo the hub nut or the friction nut on the quick release. Then fit the remover into the cut outs in the block center. Carefully check that it fits perfectly. If it does not, you could wreck both the block remover and the cut outs.

2 Once you are satisfied that everything is correct, refit the hub nut or friction nut. Do it finger tight so that it holds the block remover in place. If you have a very firmly mounted workshop vice, clamp the block remover in the jaws.

3 With the wheel in the vice, turn the rim an inch or so counterclockwise. Alternatively, use a crescent wrench to turn the remover about an inch counterclockwise. Slacken the hub nut a little, then unscrew the cluster a bit more.

4 Keep loosening the hub nut and the cluster bit by bit until it will unscrew by hand. When re-installing, spread anti-seize grease on the threads and be careful—the thread is very fine and it is only too easy to cross-thread it.

Freehubs and sprockets

8-, 9-, and 10-speed gearing can only be squeezed onto a bike by cutting down the width of the rear hub. Freehubs compensate for this loss of strength with a bearing inside the freehub body.

Freehubs pack a lot of functions into one small component, and you can only work on them if you buy three special tools, which may not be worthwhile unless you plan to change sprockets and freehub bodies frequently. It may be better to leave sprocket changes to your local bike shop.

Normal rear hubs with screw-on freewheels are being replaced by freehubs because of the extra sprockets that are now being squeezed into the narrow space—130mm for road frames, 135mm for MTB frames—between the chain stays. This means that rear hubs have to be much narrower, leaving the end of the axle unsupported on a conventional hubs. As a result, the axle can break and maybe cause an accident.

The freehub design overcomes this weakness because the freewheel mechanism is built into the hub. The gear side hub bearing can then be fitted inside the extension of the hub that carries the freehub body, with an extra one in the center of the axle in some designs. Axle breakage is therefore almost unknown on freehubs.

Bear in mind that on some early Campagnolo and Suntour freehubs, the sprockets are held on with a threaded top sprocket. In this case, the top sprocket is unscrewed using two chain whips, or a chain whip and removing tool. But both of these makers now use a lockring design, similar to the Shimano.

When they first came onto the market, only the big manufacturers like Campagnolo and Shimano made freehub sprockets, and they were pretty expensive. Now other manufacturers have climbed onto the band wagon and not only supply sprockets to install, they can also supply adapters allowing you to use Shimano sprockets on Campagnolo hubs.

To save weight, some of the largest sprockets now have an open spider design and are bolted or riveted together. Sometimes you can open up packs to change individual sprockets but take expert advice before you do so.

CHAIN WHIP

Taking off sprockets

1 Take the back wheel out of the frame, then clean up the end of the axle and the smallest sprocket. Undo the friction nut and also take the spring off the quick release.

2 Check that you have the correct removing tool. Fit the tool into the circular slot and hold it there by screwing the friction nut back onto the quick release skewer.

3 Position the chain whip on the bottom of the middle sprocket and wrap the long chain around the rest of the teeth, allowing you to exert force in a clockwise direction.

4 Rest the wheel on the floor and hold the chain whip still by pushing in a clockwise direction while you undo the sprocket lock ring counterclockwise with a large wrench.

Freehub body

1 Once you have removed the sprockets, take off the lock nut and cone on the plain side of the wheel and pull the axle out through the hub. Take the ball bearings out of the hub, and wipe off any excess grease in the working area.

2 You should now be able to see the six-sided socket in the head of the bolt that holds the freehub body to the hub itself. Check that the socket is clear and undo the bolt. You will then be able to lift the freehub body away from the hub.

3 While the freehub body is off, clean the interior surfaces of the hub and freehub body with solvent. Then apply anti-seize grease to the retaining bolt to make it easy to remove next time. Reassemble by reversing the procedure.

4 While the freehub is off the wheel, take the opportunity to clean the cassette thoroughly and flush the body through with solvent. Then oil with heavy mineral oil via the gap between the inner and outer bodies at the back.

5 It takes a lot of force to shift the lockring. Once it has moved, slacken the friction nut and the lockring bit by bit, until you can undo the lockring with your fingers.

6 As the lockring unscrews, it makes a loud cracking noise—this is perfectly normal. Finally, lift all the sprockets off and lay them down in the order that they were removed.

WHEN YOU NEED TO DO THIS JOB
◆ New sprockets may be needed if you are installing a new chain.
◆ Different size sprockets may be needed if you go climbing mountains.
◆ The freehub body may need soaking in solvent or replacing if it will not freewheel smoothly.

TIME
◆ 15 minutes to remove sprockets.
◆ 10 minutes to strip out hub axle, if necessary.
◆ 5 minutes to remove freehub body.
◆ 1 hour to put everything back together again.

DIFFICULTY
◆ One of the most difficult jobs you are likely to encounter on a bike. Removing the lockring is the most difficult, so your tools must be in good condition. The hub must be reassembled with great care.

TOOLS
◆ Appropriate lockring tool, in undamaged condition.
◆ Chain whip.
◆ Large crescent wrench.
◆ 10mm Allen key, preferably a long one.

LOCKRING TOOL

Pedals: removal and refitting

Do not underestimate the importance of the pedals. If they creak and grind as you ride along, you will never develop a smooth, efficient pedaling style. And in some cases, they can even cause knee trouble.

When they are doing the budget for a bike, makers seem to leave the choice of pedals to last, when all the money has been spent. So as a result, lots of bikes leave the factory fitted with the cheapest possible pedals, often made of nothing more than cheap plastic.

This is not good because you will never be able to pedal efficiently with pedals that do not rotate freely or broken pedals. And if the bearings suddenly seize or the cage suddenly falls apart completely, you can easily be pitched off into the road. To prevent problems, replace the pedals right away if you suspect they are unsafe.

Even when decent bearings are fitted, they are often given only a quick dab of grease at the factory and this soon gets washed away. This makes it worth stripping and greasing the pedals as a precaution, even if your bike is new or only a few months old.

Clipless pedals are removed and refitted in exactly the same way as ordinary pedals.

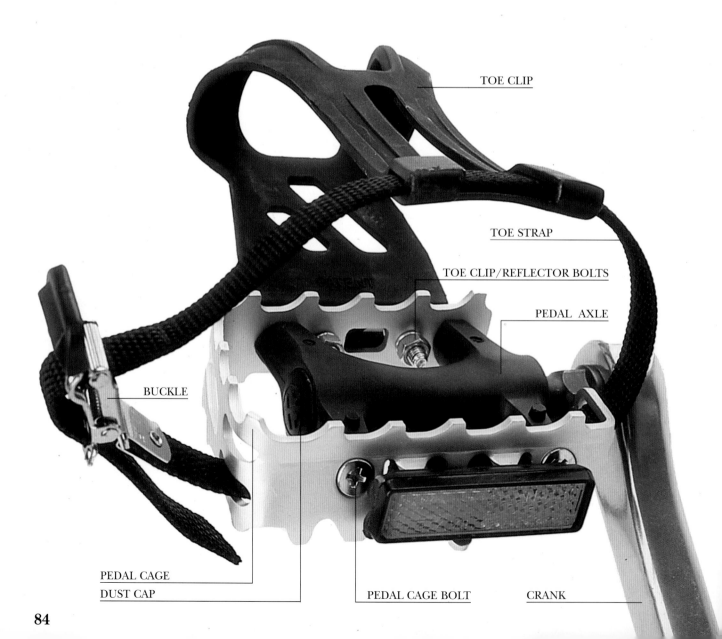

TOE CLIP

TOE STRAP

TOE CLIP/REFLECTOR BOLTS

PEDAL AXLE

BUCKLE

PEDAL CAGE

DUST CAP

PEDAL CAGE BOLT

CRANK

1 To remove the pedal on the chain side, fit a narrow 15mm or 17mm wrench onto the flats on the pedal axle. A proper wrench pedal (as in the picture) is the best tool for the job. Undo in the normal, counterclockwise direction.

2 You may find it difficult to shift the pedal. Try spraying the axle end with aerosol lube from both sides. Leave for a while and try again. If that does not work, turn the crank until the wrench is roughly parallel with the floor.

3 Hold the saddle and handlebars and put your foot onto the end of the wrench—be careful, as it will probably move suddenly. If that doesn't work, use a length of tube to extend the wrench, and try once more.

GETTING STARTED WITH PEDALS

The weight of the pedal often makes it awkward when you are trying to get the pedal thread to start screwing into the thread in the end of the crank. So use both hands, taking the weight of the pedal with one hand while you turn the axle to screw it in with the other. Vary the angle of the pedal axle to the crank a bit at a time until the pedal thread engages the thread in the crank.

4 Now for the left-hand pedal: this is very unusual because it has a left-hand thread, designed to stop it from unscrewing as you ride along. You undo a left-hand pedal by turning it clockwise—the opposite way from normal.

5 To make it easier to remove the pedals next time, coat the thread on the axle with anti-seize grease. If you do not have any anti-seize grease, use some ordinary heavy oil. This is particularly important if the cranks are made of alloy.

LOOK FOR THE HEXAGON SOCKET

Nearly all pedals have flats for a wrench on the axle. But some pedals also have a hexagon socket formed in the end of the axle—easily spotted if you look at the back of the cranks. If you are working on pedals with a hexagon socket, it is usually easier to undo the pedals with a long workshop hex key than with a wrench.

LEFT- AND RIGHT-HAND PEDALS

Pedals are nearly always marked L for Left and R for Right, on the wrench flats at the threaded part of the axle. There is a faint chance of you coming across ones marked G for gauche, meaning Left, and D for droite meaning Right.

NOTE:
Left-hand pedal: unscrew clockwise.
Right-hand pedal: unscrew counterclockwise.
Reverse direction when re-installing.

WHEN YOU NEED TO DO THIS JOB
◆ If you are installing new pedals.
◆ When stripping and greasing pedals.

TIME
◆ 5 minutes.

DIFFICULTY
◆ The most testing part is remembering about the left-hand thread.

TOOLS
◆ Long, narrow wrench, purpose-made pedal wrench, or long, Allen key.

Pedals: strip, grease, and reassemble

Though similar in principle to other bearings, pedal bearings are so small that they can be quite awkward to work on.

On a wet day, the pedals get showered with water. Most manufacturers try to stop this water getting into the pedal bearings by installing a rubber seal between the bearing and the end of the axle. This usually works quite well but it is not completely effective.

Nevertheless, when stripping down a pedal, take care to avoid damaging any rubber parts and to put them back, without twisting, in the groove or wherever else that they came from. When the seal fits into the pedal cage around the inner bearing, it is sometimes best to stick it in place with ordinary clear glue. This makes assembly easier and prevents the seal from falling out in the future.

The other way to combat water is to coat the bearings with plenty of quality, water-resistant grease. Once you have assembled and greased the pedal bearings properly, they should not need attention again for many miles. Do not worry if you find the axle or cones are slightly pitted. They will still run smoothly despite a certain amount of damage.

It is sometimes difficult to refit dust caps because they usually have a very fine thread. But if it is missing, the pedal bearings will fill with water. See if the dust cap from an old pedal will fit. If not, try temporarily covering the open end of the pedal with adhesive tape.

You will also find that smooth-turning pedals help you develop a good pedaling technique. There is no one pedaling style that works for everybody; but as a rough guideline, you should flex the ankle at the top of the pedal stroke so that the foot is positioned roughly horizontal on the down stroke. That is when you put most of the power in. Some people keep the heel slightly below the horizontal, others keep it slightly above. These variations can be sorted out by experiment and depend on your own anatomy and riding style.

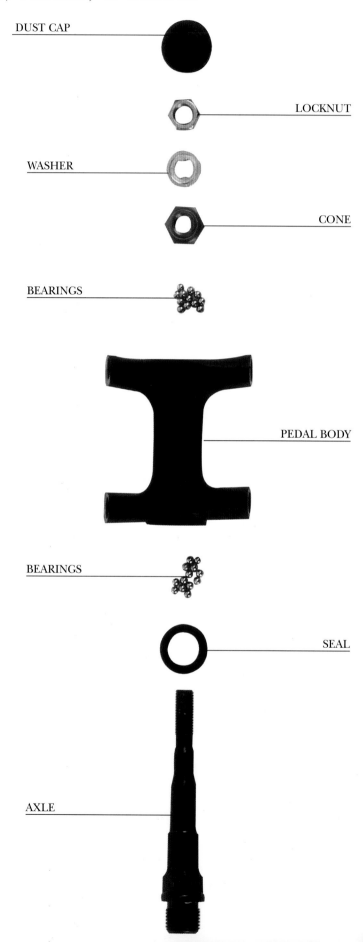

DUST CAP

LOCKNUT

WASHER

CONE

BEARINGS

PEDAL BODY

BEARINGS

SEAL

AXLE

1 Some pedals have a cage that can be separated from the pedal body. The cage certainly makes it awkward to work on pedals, so strip it off whenever possible. It may be easier if you use a vise.

2 The cage is usually fixed with Phillips or socket-head screws with countersunk heads. Loosen all four fixings a little before you remove the screws. Be careful not to distort the cage as you take it off.

3 Dust caps with domed centers are easy to pry out. But sometimes they fit flush and you have to use a tiny screwdriver. Unscrew metal dust caps with pliers or grips with wide-opening jaws.

4 Where there is a separate pedal cage, use either a socket wrench or a box wrench to undo the locknut. On many types, only a socket will reach far enough into the pedal to slacken it off.

5 Once you have loosened the locknut, you can usually undo it the rest of the way with your fingertips. If it will not come off easily, spray the axle with aerosol lube to clean the threads.

6 Take out the lock washer next. Sometimes this is quite difficult if there is a tag that fits into a groove on the axle. Try lifting it up and out with two small screwdrivers, one each side.

7 The cone is now ready to be unscrewed. If there is a slot across the face of the cone, use a screwdriver. Or slide a small screwdriver between the cone and the pedal body and force it around.

8 While unscrewing the cone, hold the axle in the pedal body with your index finger or you will get showered with greasy ball bearings. Or hold the axle in a vise by the wrench flats.

9 Catch all the loose bearings in a tin or on a piece of newspaper. Some will not drop out, so scrape them out with a pen top or similar. Clean and inspect all the minor parts, but do not worry about minor pits in the bearing surfaces.

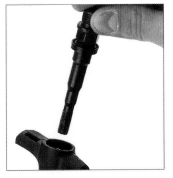

10 To re-assemble, stick the ball bearings into the inner bearing with grease, then lower the axle in. Holding the axle, turn the pedal up the other way, stick the outer bearings in, and re-fit the cone, washer, and locknut.

WHEN YOU NEED TO DO THIS JOB
◆ With new pedals, in case they are not properly greased.
◆ If the pedal bearings feel rough and gritty.
◆ When the pedal bearings are loose.

TIME
◆ 20 minutes per pedal, if you have a vise.
◆ 30 minutes per pedal if not.

DIFFICULTY
◆ There can be problems getting to the outer bearing if you cannot remove the cage from the body. Otherwise stripping the pedal bearings is very good practice for greasing and adjusting other bearings. Do not overfill with grease.

TOOLS
◆ Vise, wide-opening pliers, or slip-jointed gland pliers.

1 There are nearly always circular holes in the pedal cage for the toe clip bolts. If not, toe clips are usually supplied with a backing plate to overcome this problem. High-quality pedals often come with built-in toe clip fixings.

Toe clips, straps, and clipless pedals

Riding a bike without toe clips is a bit like riding a horse without a saddle – it can be done, but it's not really a good idea.

Riders are sometimes put off using toe clips because they feel they are unsafe. But experience shows that although it takes a little while getting used to them, clips and straps are a safety feature. On a bike with toe clips, your foot cannot slip off the pedal and cause a sudden swerve or loss of control. And if you fall off, you instinctively pull your foot out before hitting the ground.

The other advantage of toe clips is that they help you position the ball of your foot over the axle of the pedal. This makes it easier to flex your ankle at the top of the stroke, and directs all the power of your legs into the pedal.

Seldom do you need to tighten the toe straps. Most of the time, they just steady the toe clip—you only pull them tight when a major effort is needed, such as going up a steep hill. You can even buy half toe clips without straps if a 'half way house' would help you get used to toe clips.

When buying toe clips, check that you get the right size for your foot and pedal combination. When buying standard pedals, go for ones with proper toe clip mounting holes and a large tag on the back of the cage to help you pick up the pedal more easily with your foot.

Clipless pedals and the shoes that go with them come in a huge variety of designs. Not only do you need advice from an expert on a combination of shoes and pedals that will suit you, you must also make sure the shoes fit perfectly.

Clipless pedals

1 The first clipless pedals were like the bindings used on skis. A cleat on the bottom of the shoe clicks into the pedal, giving a firm connection. When it is time to get off your bike, you just twist your foot a little and it is free.

2 SPD-style clipless pedals are more compact than other types. Their best feature is the cleat 'buried' in the sole of the shoe, making it quieter and easier to walk in them. The spring clamping the shoe to the pedal can be adjusted.

2 Some road bikes are fitted with lightweight platform pedals. These are sometimes made of resin, sometimes alloy. Fit the special toe clips using the countersunk screws that come with the pedal. No nuts are needed, the holes are threaded.

3 To install nylon and leather toe straps, feed the strap through the slots cut out of the sides of the pedal cage. If tight, pull through with pliers. There is usually a special tag on the pedal cage to stop the strap from rubbing against the crank.

4 Pull the toe strap tight and position the buckle just outside the pedal cage. Leave enough slack between the buckle and the cage to slow down the pedal cutting into the strap—this is where they tend to break eventually.

5 The buckles are not intended to hold the toe strap firmly. Just pass the end under the knurled roller, then through the cut-out in the sprung part. Tighten the toe strap, when necessary, by giving the free end a jerk.

6 Installing reflectors onto the back of the pedals is particularly effective. They are almost impossible to miss by other road users because the twinkling light from the reflectors is constantly on the move. Most reflectors have a simple two-bolt attachment, similar to toe clips.

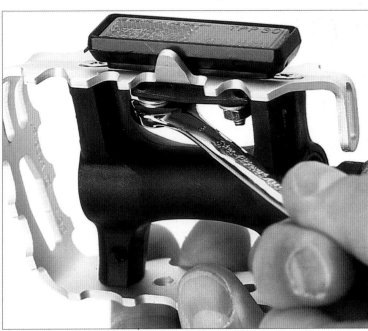

3 Mud and grit tends to clog all designs of clipless pedals, and it always takes a second or so to click the shoe into place. To make it easier to use clipless pedals, double-sided designs with a frame are now used on many MTBs.

4 You can only use clipless pedals with shoes that have screw fixings for the cleats built into the sole. Some SPD shoes are fine for use on ordinary pedals but cleats can be fitted by simply cutting out an area of the rubber sole.

WHEN YOU NEED TO DO THIS JOB
◆ When equipping a new bike.
◆ Getting the bike ready for winter.

TIME
◆ 15 minutes to install toe clips and straps.
◆ 5 minutes to install reflectors.

DIFFICULTY
◆ No real problems, but you will sometimes find that the toe straps are very tight in the slots.

Chainrings and cranks

If you are not sure which type of drivetrain and bottom bracket you are dealing with, refer back to the beginning of this chapter.

Alloy cotterless cranksets are fitted to the vast majority of recent bikes. In most cases, these have replaceable chainrings. Very handy if wear reaches the point at which new chainrings are needed, or if you want to radically change the gearing. However, manufacturers are not always keen on supplying chainrings on their own and they only offer a very limited number of variations.

Instead, you may have to ask your dealer to get hold of one from a specialist supplier. The French firm TA is the best known and they can supply chainrings to install almost any crank and with almost any number of teeth. Bear in mind that not only do the number of fixing bolts vary, so does the pitch circle diameter (PCD). The PCD is the diameter of a circle joining all the fixing bolts. Campagnolo now use a PCD of 135mm but most Shimano cranks have a 130mm PCD.

Normally, chainrings can be bolted to the spider in any position, but with the oval type that was popular a few years ago, and with many Shimano transmissions, the chainring must be fitted in a set position in relation to the crank. Check for marks on the back of the chainring and spider, and assemble accordingly. If there is a pin on the outer face of the large chainring, this must be positioned behind the crank arm to prevent the chain from getting stuck between the chainring and crank.

Early types of cotterless cranks were fixed to the bottom bracket axle with an ordinary looking hexagon-headed bolt. These cranks are fitted and removed with a special extractor tool. Later types have socket-head crank bolts that should be done up very tight with a long hex key. Better yet, use a torque wrench. This ensures the cranks are correctly tightened, a point that will come up very quickly if you ever try to claim warranty.

Socket-head bolts are still used on the latest cranks, which fit onto a pipe billet axle. The end of the axle is a different shape, which gives a more secure fixing but the 8 mm hex-headed crank fixing bolts must be done up much tighter than earlier types. The axle is machined out of a hollow length of pipe to save weight.

Cottered cranksets used to be found on most budget utility bikes—but even some of these are now fitted with steel cotterless cranksets. Nevertheless, you can still buy new cotter pins if the old ones get damaged. But remember, there are different types and sizes of cotter pin, so take the old one along as a pattern.

The third type of drivetrain has both cranks and the axle all in one piece. These are installed on kids' bikes, budget BMX, and budget adult utility bikes. See page 99 for servicing instructions.

Smear anti-seize grease onto the threads of all nuts and bolts used to fix chainrings to crank spiders and other chainrings.

Removing chainrings

1 Nearly all chainrings are bolted to the crank spider with chrome socket head bolts. Undo the first bolt half -a- turn, then the next one half -a- turn, continuing like that until all of the fixing bolts are loose enough to undo by hand.

2 The socket head bolt shown fits into a sleeve nut that extends through all three chainrings plus the crank spider. Pull off the outer ring by pulling gently on opposite sides—it is a tight fit to prevent unwanted movement.

Removing socket bolt cranks

1 First, undo the outer cap with a pin spanner. Then wind the crank fixing bolt in a counterclockwise direction with a long 7- or 8-mm hex key. Stop the cranks moving with your other hand.

2 Pull the crank a little to finally detach it from the axle. In this case, a pipe billet bottom bracket unit is installed but you are more likely to find a standard bottom bracket with a square spline fitting.

3 Check for spacers or washers between the chainrings, then lift the outer ring away for cleaning or straightening. The other rings usually remain in place until you draw the sleeve nuts out of the holes in the cranks.

4 In some cases, the small inner ring is bolted in place with a separate ring of bolts. Undo them all and the inner ring will come off. You may find that the smallest ring is made of steel so that it does not wear out too quickly.

WHEN YOU NEED TO DO THIS JOB
◆ Chainrings are worn or bent.
◆ Bottom bracket bearings need checking.

TIME
◆ 20 minutes for chainrings.
◆ 10 minutes to remove socket bolt cranks.

DIFFICULTY ✦✦✦✦
◆ Changing a chainring requires care to prevent bending or distortion. Removing socket bolt cranks is easier than other cotterless types.

SPECIAL TOOLS
◆ Extractor tool not required to remove socket bolt cranks.

3 Collect the protective outer cap, the crank fixing bolt, and narrow washer so that you do not lose them. The washer sits in the recess in the crank, so you may have to pick it out with your fingernail.

4 Check that the bottom bracket is running silently and smoothly, then carefully clean all the old grease off the minor parts. Regrease the fixing bolt and washer with quality non-lithium grease.

5 Locate the crank on the end of the bottom bracket axle, slip the washer in the crank recess, and fit the crank fixing bolt. Tighten the crank bolt with a torque wrench to the maker's specified figure.

6 Screw the outer cap on top of the crank fixing bolt with your finger tips, then tighten it up with a pin wrench. When a pipe billet bracket is fitted, take care to install the other crank exactly opposite the first one.

TORQUE WRENCH
Bike and component makers now say that you should always use a torque wrench when fitting a nut or bolt. Torque wrenches measure the amount of force being applied to a nut or bolt via a standard socket wrench. The sockets fit on the torque wrench in the usual way but the ⅜in size is best for bikes. A certain amount of force is set down for each individual nut and bolt on a list in the maker's handbook. When tightened to the force specified, nuts and bolts should never break or come loose. The attraction for manufacturers is that if they are faced with a warranty claim, they can reject it unless the claimant can show that a torque wrench was used when working on the part.

Crank removal

Taking off cotterless cranks can be nerve-racking, but once you have done it a couple of times without problems, you are on your way to becoming a good mechanic.

The bottom bracket axle for most cotterless cranks is accurately ground into a tapered shape called a spline. This four-sided spline, as well as the tapered hole in the crank that fits onto it, has to be made very accurately. Axle splines are nearly all the same size, whatever the maker.

When reinstalling, reverse the process for removal, assembling the crank and axle with the lightest possible coating of grease on the surfaces where they touch. This prevents corrosion between the steel axle and the alloy crank which makes it easier to get the cranks off later. Some people also like to tap the cranks home lightly with a soft mallet, or a hammer with a piece of wood as a cushion.

Once installed, tighten the crank bolts up as hard as you can. The extractor tool usually has a socket wrench for this part of the job, but you can get more leverage if you use a socket and ratchet handle from a normal $^3/_8$in socket set.

You should also tighten up the bolt every hundred miles or so for the first few hundred miles, in case the crank bolt loosens under pressure.

Do not ride a bike with a loose crank because the hard steel axle easily damages the soft alloy. Once it has been damaged, it may not be possible to stop a crank from coming loose. If your cranks just will not stay tight, try using Loctite stud adhesive on the spline. If that does not work, you may be able to get a spare crank from your bike shop.

Cranks with ordinary bolts

1 Undo the dust cap. Next, loosen the crank bolt by turning the wrench on the extractor tool counterclockwise with an open-ended wrench. If the wrench is not a tight fit, use a $^3/_8$in socket instead.

2 Undo the crank bolt the rest of the way with your fingers, then pull it out. Check that you do not leave the large washer behind or it could prevent the extractor tool from working properly later.

COTTERED CRANKSET WITH BOTTOM BRACKET

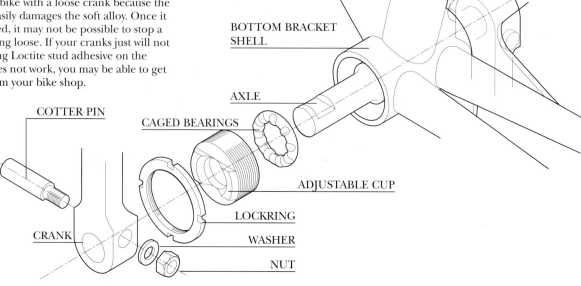

BOTTOM BRACKET SHELL

AXLE

COTTER PIN

CAGED BEARINGS

ADJUSTABLE CUP

LOCKRING

CRANK

WASHER

NUT

3 Get ready to remove the crank by checking that the thread on the extractor tool and the internal thread around the crank bolt recess are clean and undamaged. Slowly screw the extractor into the thread.

4 Check that the extractor is going in straight. If it seems to tighten up after the first couple of turns, the extractor is probably going in at an angle. Take it out and screw it in again more carefully.

5 When you are sure the extractor is installed correctly, tighten the extractor bolt. You will find it takes quite a lot of force to push the crankset off the axle at first. Hold one crank stationary as you work.

WHEN YOU NEED TO DO THIS JOB
◆ For access to the bottom bracket.
◆ When the bike needs a thorough overhaul.

TIME
◆ Allow 30 minutes the first time, so that you can check carefully as you go.
◆ 10 minutes once you are used to the job.

DIFFICULTY
◆ You need a delicate touch when screwing the extractor into the crank, and quite a lot of force when actually pushing the crank off the axle.

TOOLS
◆ Correct crank extractor with undamaged threads. A socket set may also be useful.

Cottered crankset

1 Remove the nut and washer on the cotter pin, then give it one sharp blow with a mechanic's hammer. If that does not fire the cotter pin right out, find a 1in diameter metal bar, place on the pin, and hammer on that instead.

2 You can re-use the old cotter pin if it is not damaged. If you have to install a new cotter, take the old one to the bike shop as a pattern. When you are ready to reinstall the crankset, test-fit the new cotter pin and see how well it fits.

3 Slip the washer on the threaded end of the new cotter pin and tighten the nut as far as it will go by hand. If there isn't enough thread to reach the end of the nut, file some metal off the flat part. Repeat, if necessary.

4 Install the cotter pin so the nut is under the crank when the crank points backward. Bash it right home with a medium hammer, then install the washer. Tighten the nut hard with a wrench. Install the other cotter the opposite way.

Cartridge bottom brackets

The most heavily loaded bearing on a bike is the bottom bracket, so a better bottom bracket unit is a big step forward.

Many new bikes are equipped with a sealed or cartridge bottom bracket at the factory. This speeds up assembly and has the additional advantage that the seals around the axle keep out water almost completely. And instead of loose ball bearings, the axle is supported on proper ball or roller bearings.

This means that a sealed bottom bracket usually lasts a lot longer than an ordinary one. But once a sealed bracket starts to wear, that is it. They cannot be greased or adjusted—ou just have to install a new one.

Sealed brackets can be fitted to almost any bike with a cotterless crankset as an upgrade. No modifications to the bottom bracket shell or frame are required, although slots to let water drain away are provided on some frames.

Sealed bottom brackets are supplied by crankset manufacturers and by many independent makers. Some produce extremely light but expensive units made out of titanium and other fancy materials. Others produce original equipment-quality ones, often more cheaply than the big makers. The main variable when buying spares is the length of the axle. This depends on the number of chainrings, plus the design of the cranks and the frame. Do not worry about the four-sided spline because most are the same size. Always take the old unit to your bike shop for reference.

Road riders only need to touch a cartridge bottom bracket every few thousand miles. Mountain bikers may have to change a sealed bottom bracket more frequently.

If you find that the threads in the bottom bracket shell are tight, clean them up with aerosol lube and by screwing an old bottom bracket cup in and out a few times. Cut a vertical hacksaw slot in the bearing cup to help get rid of any dirt in the threads.

Pipe billet axles

1 Clean inside the bottom bracket with aerosol lube, then lightly coat the threads with grease. Fit the special tool in the recess around the axle and screw the unit in counterclockwise from the chain side.

2 Switching to the non-chain side of the bike, screw the collar or adapter into the bottom bracket shell in a clockwise direction with your fingers. Check that it goes in absolutely straight.

3 Tighten the sealed unit into position using the removal tool and wrench. It is fully home when the edge of the threaded portion is flush with the edge of the bottom bracket shell. It screws in counterclockwise.

4 Finally, from the non-chain side, tighten the collar clockwise until it meets the end of the cartridge, locking it into place. When fully tight, the collar will be almost invisible, hidden in the bracket shell.

ASSEMBLY VARIATIONS
The sealed unit shown on page 95 is a budget version from Shimano. Here the collar is installed from the drive side but many other types, including later Shimano, are assembled the opposite way, with the collar screwed in from the non-chain side. If you have trouble fitting a sealed unit, check in case you should be installing it from the other side. Check also whether it is a left-hand or a right-hand thread.

Square axles

1 With the bottom bracket tool slotted into the collar, fit a big crescent wrench onto the hexagon and turn clockwise. This should undo the collar that locks the sealed unit into the bottom bracket shell.

2 Use minimum force on the wrench, as the collar on cheaper types is made of a resin-based plastic. Even the collars made of aluminum are fairly fragile. Remember to undo clockwise, not as normal.

3 Now move to the opposite side of the bike, and again fit the removal tool. In this case, you unscrew the cartridge in the normal, counterclockwise direction. This is not as tricky as removing the collar.

4 The unit can now be pulled out of the bottom bracket shell. Check that the rubber axle seals, where visible, are in good condition, and that the axle revolves smoothly and easily. Clean the threads.

5 Clean up the inside of the bracket also with a squirt of aerosol lube. Screw the collar in counterclockwise with your fingers, from the drive side, to check that the threads are clean. Remove, then screw the cartridge back into the bracket shell, and lock it in place with the collar. Coat all the threads with anti-seize grease as you go.

WHEN YOU NEED TO DO THIS JOB
◆ Upgrading from a standard bottom bracket.
◆ Installing a new crankset.

TIME
◆ 40 minutes—mainly because you have to clean up the threads.

DIFFICULTY
◆ Calls for the same combination of delicacy and force as when removing cotterless cranks.

TOOLS
◆ Bracket tool, long wrench, old bottom bracket cups.

SEALED BOTTOM BRACKET
A complete sealed or cartridge bottom bracket consists of the main body, usually with a metal casing, and two separate collars that hold the sealed unit in the bottom bracket shell. The collars always have provision for engaging with some form of bottom bracket remover.

Cup and axle bottom bracket: 1

One standard bottom bracket may look very different from another but they all strip down in exactly the same way.

Standard bottom brackets need fairly regular maintenance. Once a month is not too often for a bike used seriously off-road, once a year is the absolute minimum for a road bike used frequently. But unlike most bike components, it is easy to ignore the bottom bracket until it has almost seized up.

The main problem with cup and axle bottom brackets is water penetration. The movement of the bearings churns the grease, oil, and water into a sticky mess that does very little lubricating.

If you are lucky, the bottom bracket will develop a regular squeak, telling you that something is wrong. By that time, however, the bearing tracks in the cups will probably be pitted and some of the hardening will have worn off the axle. This will show up as an area of small pits, where the underlying metal is a different color.

If you find any of these problems, install new parts. Luckily you can install a new axle with old cups; or new cups with an old axle; or even mix different makes of axle and cups. The only point to watch out for is that Italian frames often have a different thread in the bottom bracket shell.

Final adjustment is easier if you install the chainring and crank first, and then screw the adjustable cup in or out until you can feel only a slight movement at the end of the crank. If you tighten the lockring at this point, it will pull the adjustable cup out slightly. This is often enough to make up for the way the adjustable cup usually turns slightly when you finally tighten the lockring.

When you strip a bracket, you may find eleven separate bearings, or the bearings may be in a cage. Both arrangements work fine but separate ball bearings are probably better because the load is shared between a larger number of bearings.

Strip and overhaul

1 After removing the cranks, start work on the non-chain side. If the lockring has a series of square cut-outs, find a suitable drift or cold chisel that roughly fits them. Then, with an ball peen hammer, tap the lockring counterclockwise.

2 As you tap the lockring, it may drag the adjustable cup around with it. After a turn or two, you should be able to unscrew the bearing cup with your fingers. Catch any loose ball bearings as you remove the cup, followed by

5 When you re-install the bearing cups, only the grease stops the ball bearings from falling out. Once all eleven are in place, cover them with more grease, but scoop out any surplus that spills over into the hole for the axle with the same pen top.

6 Screw the fixed cup into the drive side, tightening it counterclockwise as hard as you can. Steady the axle with your fingers and thread the longer side of the axle, if there is one, into the fixed cup. The shorter side fits into the adjustable cup.

3 Moving to the drive side now. The main problem is finding an crescent wrench large enough for the flats on a fixed cup. Once you've found one, undo the fixed cup in a clockwise direction, but be careful not to chip the paint.

4 Clean everything up with solvent and inspect all the bearing surfaces. If they are fine, half fill the cups with waterproof grease and add eleven ball bearings per side. A pen top is fine for pressing the ball bearings into the grease.

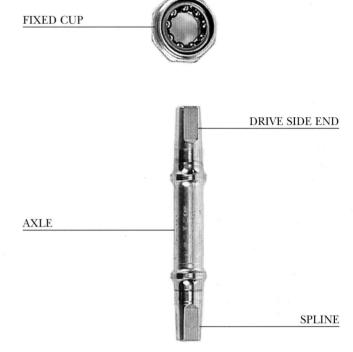

FIXED CUP

DRIVE SIDE END

AXLE

SPLINE

7 Screw in the adjustable cup until it tightens up. Turn the axle and if it feels tight, loosen the adjustable cup until the gravelly feeling goes away. Install and tighten the lockring, check that the axle turns smoothly, and re-adjust if necessary.

WHEN YOU NEED TO DO THIS JOB
◆ To stop a squeak.
◆ During a full overhaul.
◆ At least once a year.

TIME
◆ Best part of 1 hour.

DIFFICULTY
◆ Getting the fixed cup in and out is a problem if you do not have exactly the right tools. In addition, you tend to lose the adjustment when you tighten the lock ring at the end of the job.

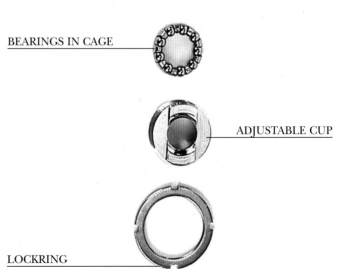

BEARINGS IN CAGE

ADJUSTABLE CUP

LOCKRING

Cup and axle bottom bracket: 2

Specialized tools make it much easier to overhaul and adjust a cup and axle bottom bracket.

Fixed bottom bracket cups are not easy to work on. Not only do you have to remember that they have a left-hand thread, so they tighten up counterclockwise; you also have to cope with their tight fit in the bracket shell to stop them from coming loose.

You can tighten up a fixed cup with a crescent wrench or a set of channel locks, but either way you are quite likely to chip the paint. A fixed cup bottom bracket wrench will make it easier to fit and remove them, but you still have to be very careful to prevent the wrench from slipping off the narrow rim of the bearing cup.

The adjustable cup often has two holes on the face so that you can screw it in or out with a pin spanner. Then, when doing the final adjustment, you can use the pin spanner to hold the bearing cup still while you tighten the lockring with a C-wrench. Remember, you have to hit the point where the axle turns freely but without any free play. A C-wrench can also be used in conjunction with an open-ended wrench on hexagonally shaped bottom brackets.

Using bottom bracket wrenches

1 The best fixed bottom bracket wrenches fit right round the outside of the bearing cup. If you operate the wrench with one hand and push it onto the bearing cup with the other, you minimize the chances of it slipping and damaging the paintjob.

2 When adjusting a standard bracket, it is best to tighten the lockring with a C-wrench. Fit the dog on the wrench into a notch in the lockring and steady your hand on the frame. In this case, you can use an open-ended wrench on the adjusting cup.

LOST BEARINGS
Look out for these basic faults when you are deciding whether to install new parts. On the left-hand bearing cup above, the chrome has flaked off and the bearing track is covered in tiny pits. The right-hand cup is worn all over and in some areas, the surface of the metal has been worn away. On the axles, the upper one has many small pits while on the lower one, the hardened surface is worn through and the soft metal underneath is crumbling fast.

One piece cranks

This design is mainly used on kids' bikes but also on budget BMXs and adult utilities. Although designed to keep down the cost of building small bikes, one piece cranks and the bottom bracket design that goes with them are surprisingly child-resistant. The cranks can get bent in a crash but they are made of steel, so if you have a big pair of channel locks, you can usually straighten them up without much difficulty. If the left-hand crank gets badly bent, consider taking the whole thing apart and straightening it in a vise.

The bottom bracket works well because it is a lot bigger in diameter than a standard one and it contains more ball bearings to share the load. The press-in bearing cups and the axle can get pitted but do not have to be replaced unless the cups are very badly damaged. Maintenance consists of removing the old grease, regreasing everything, and fitting it back together with a full set of ball bearings.

It is worth going through this procedure as a precaution, if you have just bought a second-hand bike. And judging by the way kids' bikes are often thrown

1 First thing is to remove the pedals, then unscrew the lockring in a clockwise direction. The lockring is very thin, so steady the wrench to prevent it slipping off the flats. Once you have unscrewed it all the way, lift the lockring off the end of the crank.

2 Behind the lockring is a slotted bearing retainer. Position a cold chisel in the slot and tap it gently in a clockwise direction. As you unscrew the retainer, the crank assembly will tilt, so support it with one hand while you undo the retainer with the other.

3 Lift the bearing retainer off the end of the crank. If you then tilt the whole assembly until the plain crank is almost horizontal, you can draw it out of the opposite side of the bottom bracket shell. The crank assembly is made of steel and is quite heavy.

4 Finally, knock the bearing cups out of the frame. They are not threaded but are still a tight fit. When one side of the cup has moved a little, swap the cold chisel to the opposite side and hammer away until it also moves, otherwise the cups will jam in place.

together in the factory, it would not be a bad idea to strip and grease the bottom bracket on a new bike as well.

It is not easy to get spares for this type of bike, so wait until you have got them in your hand before you strip the bike down. If your

local bike shop cannot supply the correct parts, search out a specialist in kids bikes.

To refit the bottom bracket, follow the steps given here in reverse. But take care to tap the bearing cups back in straight, not at an angle, or you will never get them in.

WHEN YOU NEED TO DO THIS JOB

◆You have just bought a second-hand or new bike and want to check that the bottom bracket is OK.
◆ There is a grinding noise as you turn the cranks.
◆ The cranks have been bent in a crash.

TIME

At least an hour to strip, clean, and refit the whole assembly. Longer if you have to straighten the cranks as well.

DIFFICULTY ✦✦✦✦

At first it is difficult to see how this assembly fits together. Once you have grasped that, you may also have problems driving out and refitting the bearing cups. The answer is to only drive one side out a little way first. Then go to the opposite side of the bearing cup and drive that out an equal amount so it is kept straight.

SPECIAL TOOLS

Large crescent wrench, ball peen hammer, and cold chisel.

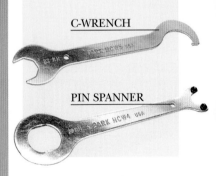

C-WRENCH

PIN SPANNER

CHAPTER 6

BRAKING SYSTEMS

The brakes are one of the most critical systems on your bike. So, in the interest of safety, set up a regular routine based on tightening all the nuts and bolts up firmly, checking alignment of the brake pads after every job and then double-checking everything, just in case.

Types of brakes

Nearly all new MTBs are equipped with V brakes, although there are millions of standard cantilevers still around. Road bikes are equipped with several different designs but dual pivots are best for most riders.

Although there are several different designs, most braking systems work by pressing a pad against the braking surface on the wall of the wheel rim. How well this works depends on how hard the pad is forced against the rim, how flat the braking surface of the rim is, and how well the pad material bites on it.

Brake pads wear fairly fast but do not forget that the braking surface of a wheel rim also wears. However, if the pad material is compatible with the material the rim is made of, this only happens very slowly. If you buy pads without checking with the dealer, they could be incompatible. In that case, the wall of the rim will wear away much more quickly and there is a danger of the wheel collapsing without warning.

To prevent this from happening, check the condition of the braking surface when you install new pads and occasionally during normal use. Have the wheel rebuilt with a new rim as soon as the wear gets beyond the stage of shallow grooves. A truly flat braking surface improves braking considerably, so consider installing rims with a machined braking surface.

CANTILEVER BRAKE
Installed on mountain bikes, hybrids, and a few road machines. A sound design that has now been overtaken by V brakes. Nevertheless, standard cantis combine low weight, powerful stopping, and plenty of clearance for mud.

CENTER PULL BRAKES
No longer made, but millions are still in use because they can be quite powerful and need little maintenance. Two separate brake arms are fitted to the backplate so, if fitted correctly, the brake pads are always evenly spaced from the wheel rim.

DUAL PIVOT BRAKES
A big advance in brakes for road bikes. Each brake arm moves independently on a separate backplate. Once correctly set up, the brake pads stay at an equal distance from the wheel rim, without constant fiddling. Most dual pivot calipers are 49mm deep but some 57mm deep ones are available.

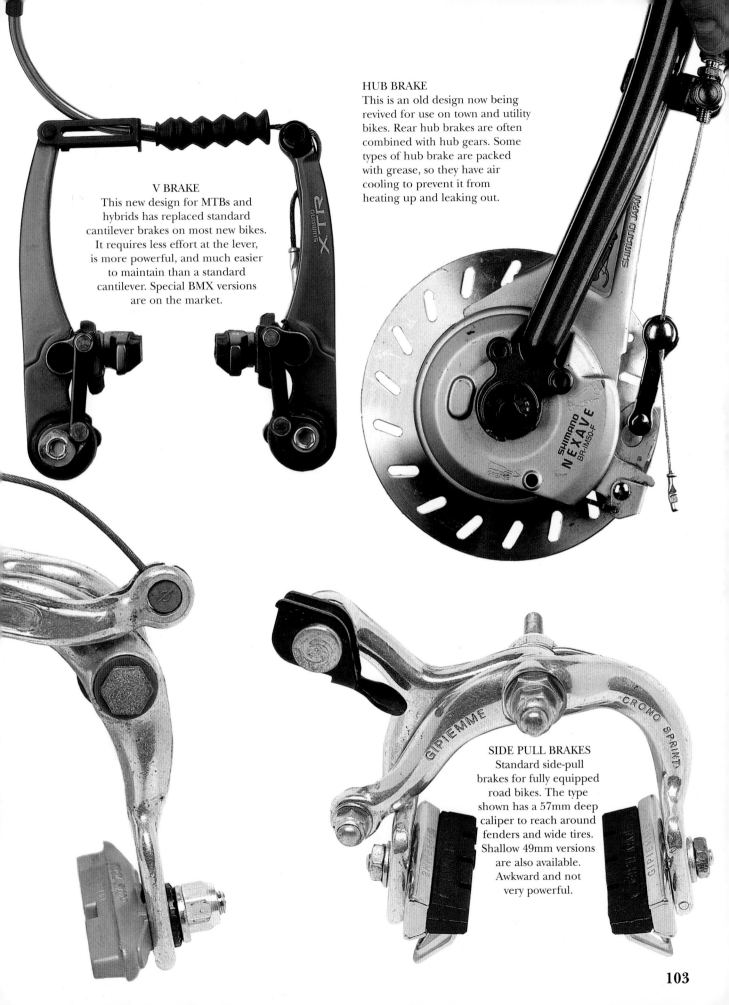

V BRAKE
This new design for MTBs and hybrids has replaced standard cantilever brakes on most new bikes. It requires less effort at the lever, is more powerful, and much easier to maintain than a standard cantilever. Special BMX versions are on the market.

HUB BRAKE
This is an old design now being revived for use on town and utility bikes. Rear hub brakes are often combined with hub gears. Some types of hub brake are packed with grease, so they have air cooling to prevent it from heating up and leaking out.

SIDE PULL BRAKES
Standard side-pull brakes for fully equipped road bikes. The type shown has a 57mm deep caliper to reach around fenders and wide tires. Shallow 49mm versions are also available. Awkward and not very powerful.

Brakes: inspection and lube

Pad wear causes a gradual fall in braking performance, so test your brakes frequently in case you do not notice the slow deterioration.

There is nearly always a lot of give when you pull the brake lever. Some of it is cable stretch, the lever itself also flexes a little, and so do the brake arms. However, brake arms should be quite stiff and if you notice that they flex more than a millimeter or two, consider upgrading to better-quality brakes. If you have standard cantis, that usually means relacing them with V brakes.

Road bike brake arms are longer and thinner, so they usually flex more than cantilevers. Side pull brakes also move off-center at the drop of a hat, often allowing the brake pad to touch the rim. Dual pivots do not suffer from this problem and this is the upgrade path for racers and sports bikes.

If you notice that you bring the brake levers fairly close to the handlebars when braking normally, maybe cable stretch and pad wear have built up to the point where servicing is overdue.

Test, inspect, and adjust

1 Test the brakes by pulling the brake lever. It will not take much effort at first, then the pads will hit the rim, and when you pull harder, it will just stretch the cable. If the brake lever ends up anywhere near the handlebar, adjustment is needed urgently.

2 First, check for worn brake pads and for contamination on the surface and wear ridges as well. If the slots are nearly worn away or the wear line has almost gone, install new pads. Do the same if you cannot remove the contamination or the ridges are cut deep into the rubber.

Brake lubrication

1 If the frame has slotted cable stops, pull the inner cable through the slot and fire lube down the outer cable. If not, just lube the inner cable. On standard cantilevers, aim one shot of lube at the back of the brake boss, where it will protect the spring from rust.

2 Standard cantis need another shot for the front of the pivots (double arrow) and just a drip on the free end of the straddle cable. This is to prevent it from getting stuck in its slot. Remember that the brake levers also need a shot of spray lube on the pivot.

QUICK RELEASE
If the quick release does not work or is missing, try turning the cable adjuster as far clockwise as possible. That should slacken off the cable enough to let you remove the wheel. If it is still not possible to remove the wheel, try letting the tire down. When installing new cables, it is a good idea to set the adjuster in the middle of its travel so that you can use it as a quick release, if necessary.

3 Now adjust the cables. On cantis and V brakes, the cable adjuster is on the brake lever. Undo the thin locknut using pliers if it is stiff. Give the adjuster two counterclockwise turns, but always leave three full threads in the lever for safety to prevent it from falling out.

4 Test and re-adjust the cable until total brake lever travel is about 20mm. On most road bikes, you again undo the locknut, then follow the procedure in step 3. You may have to loosen the cable clamp and pull some cable through to tighten the cable enough.

3 The cables and brake levers on V brakes need the same treatment as standard cantis. The pivots need a squirt of lube on each side of the brake arm and so does the slotted link between the pivot and pad, where fitted. Finally, give the cable holder a shot, as well.

4 Side pull brakes have a lot of internal friction, so give the central pivot and spring a good squirt of lube. If the brakes feel heavy, unbolt from the frame. If a lot of effort is needed to squeeze the arms together, clean and lube the caliper, then install a new cable.

Quick releases

Most braking systems have a quick release device to increase the pad clearance when removing a wheel.

BRAKE RELEASE BUTTON

1 On some high-quality road bikes, the quick release button is on the brake lever. Push it in for more clearance. It re-sets automatically when you next use the brakes.

2 On cantilevers, squeeze the brake arms together with one hand while you unhook the loose end of the straddle wire with the other. If it will not budge, slacken the cable off with the adjuster so that the tire will pass between the brake pads.

3 V brakes have a somewhat awkward quick release. First grasp the top of the brake arms and squeeze them together. Then try to steady the cable holder with your thumb while you pull and lift the cable pipe and cable away from the cable holder. You have to lift the inner cable out of a narrow slot in the cable holder, so do not use force.

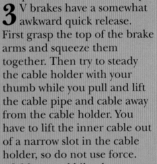

4 Most road bikes have a quick release near the cable adjuster. You pull it upward when changing the wheel and push it downward to close the pads up against the rim. Sometimes, you turn the cable holder through ninety degrees.

WHEN YOU NEED TO DO THIS JOB
◆ Every 500 miles (800km) and whenever you do a minor service.
◆ There is a lot of brake lever travel when braking normally.

TIME
◆ 5 minutes to adjust and lube the brakes.
◆ 5 minutes to tighten the cable.

DIFFICULTY ⚒⚒
◆ Luckily it is very easy to keep your brakes in good working order, so there is no excuse for neglecting them.

V and Hub brakes

Few bike components have ever had the instant impact of V brakes. Very high priced to begin with, within a matter of months they had swept all other designs from the market through sheer excellence.

V brakes are close relatives of the standard cantilever but solve pretty well all the problems of the ordinary canti. They are light enough to operate with two fingers, because the extended brake arms give more leverage. Installation and adjustment is easier because there is only one cable. And they are more powerful, partly because of the extra leverage and partly because the brake cable works at ninety degrees to the brake arms. This gives a very direct or linear pull.

Luckily, it is easy to upgrade to V brakes, provided your frame is equipped with brake bosses 80 mm from center to center. Check this measurement if the bosses look bent or you cannot get them to work well.

You cannot use the old brake levers because they are designed for brakes that need a long pull for maximum braking power. You have to use brake levers designed for direct pull brakes, which usually means brake levers that are specially designed for V brakes. There is only one more warning—and that is you must use V brakes very gently to start with. They stop you so fast, compared with ordinary bike brakes, that they can have you inadvertently diving over the handlebars.

The instructions here cover installation for the brake arms only. For installing new cables, see page 114. And for adjusting brake pads, see page 118.

Strictly speaking, V brakes are made by Shimano only. Similar designs by other manufacturers are known as long-arm cantilever or 'linear pull' brakes.

Hub brakes are staging a slight comeback on utility and city bikes because they are clean, very powerful and work equally well in all weather. The drawbacks are that you have to have them regreased every six months and that they weigh more.

Cable adjustment is very easy, but if you have any problem getting hold of new cables, try a motor bike shop. Should you ever see grease leaking out of the brake, or hear odd squealing or grinding noises, take the bike back to the dealer without delay. The six-month regreasing is also a job for the dealer. However, this is almost the only maintenance required because the brake shoes are made of steel.

1 Most V brakes are operated by combined gear and brake levers. There is a normal cable adjuster, but Servo Wave brake levers also have a device to alter the amount of pull needed. Do not alter this setting.

6 Lubricate the cable pipe and pull the inner cable through until the slack is taken up. Fit the inner through the slot in the cable holder and position the end of the cable pipe in the cable holder as well. Pull the inner cable tight.

HUB BRAKES

To adjust a hub brake, try to prop the bike up so that the wheel is right off the ground. Then tighten the cable with the adjuster so that you can feel the brake binding when you spin the wheel. Next, back off the brake about half a turn clockwise of the cable adjuster. The back wheel should now spin without any drag at all. If there is still some drag, turn the cable adjuster clockwise a fraction. Finally, check that the brake comes on fully, well before the brake lever hits the handlebar.

2 First of all, test-fit the brake arms on the pivots. If they seem tight, remove any paint or polish the metal with a light abrasive and test again. Once the brake arms move easily on the brake bosses, but without any slop, apply a little grease.

3 Each brake arm has a small coil spring with a stopper pin on the end. Fit this pin into the middle hole of the boss–do not use the other two. Then push the brake arm onto the brake boss and screw the fixing bolt into place.

4 Make sure that the long part of the spring is on the frame side of the brake arm, where it sits up against a metal stop. Next, tighten the fixing bolt, which presses the brake arm onto the brake boss and then reinstall the other brake arm.

5 Flip open the cable end cover (arrow in step 1) on the brake lever, push the plain end of the inner cable through the brake lever and adjuster, then the outer cable. Finally, feed the rear brake inner cable through the metal cable pipe.

7 Slide the cable bellows onto the inner cable and thread the end into the cable clamp. Rotate the brake arms into an upright position and check that there is 39mm or a little more inner cable showing between the brake arms.

8 Tighten the cable clamp but not fully yet. Adjust the brake pads as explained on page 118, making sure that there is an equal gap between the pad and the rim each side. The pad to rim gap should only be about 2mm in total.

9 Fully tighten the cable clamp and use the cable adjuster on the brake lever to set the total pad-to-rim gap at around 2mm. Finally, use the tiny Phillips or socket head screws on the brake arms to equalize the pad-to-rim gap.

WHEN YOU NEED TO DO THIS JOB
◆ When upgrading from standard cantis.
◆ The grease on the brake bosses has dried up.

TIME
◆ Two hours to remove old brakes, clean up brake bosses, and reinstall both new brakes.

DIFFICULTY
◆ It can be tricky getting the brake arms as upright as possible, while keeping the 39mm distance between them. Otherwise this job is straightforward.

BRAKE MODULATION
Brake modulators are found on quite a few recent bikes. Some modulators are built into the brake lever, as on the Shimano Servo Wave brake lever for V brakes. Others are installed on the brake arm, and others are part of the brake cable on some children's bikes. It is said that by adjusting the modulator, you can choose exactly the amount of power that the brake will produce and the length of pull needed on the lever. However, the real reason for installing modulators is to enable bike manufacturers to buy only one type of lever and use it with various types of brakes. Probably the best thing to do is to leave the modulator alone unless you have very definite reasons for fiddling with it.

Cantilever brake: overhaul and adjustment

The short, stiff arms of cantilever brakes generate plenty of reliable stopping power. You only need to strip them down when rust or mud has gotten into the brake bosses and stopped them from working properly.

The original type of cantilever brake has a straddle cable that joins the two arms and which is connected to the main brake cable by a metal yoke. This set up works well and is still used by some manufacturers.

Many Shimano cantilevers have a different arrangement. In this design, the main brake cable passes through a cable carrier and is connected directly to one of the brake arms. The other arm is connected to the cable carrier by a short link wire.

Some types of Shimano cantis have the pad mounted on the other side of the brake arm from the one in the drawing. This brings the pad closer to the pivot, reducing vibration and smoothing out the braking. There is no other difference.

Link wire types are harder to set up but give you better control over, and better modulation of, the amount of braking. However, when you are working on any type of cantilever brake, use the adjustment procedure given here together with the advice on installing new cables on page 110.

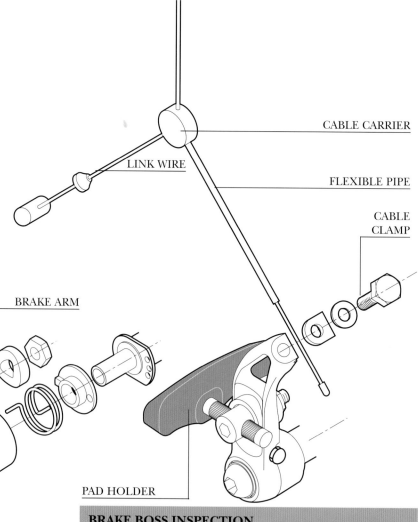

CABLE CARRIER

LINK WIRE

FLEXIBLE PIPE

CABLE CLAMP

BRAKE ARM

PAD HOLDER

BRAKE PAD

BRAKE BOSS INSPECTION
When you strip down standard cantis or V brakes, always inspect the brake bosses on the frame. If they are rusty, polish with an emery cloth and reassemble with waterproof grease on the brake bosses. Check that the bosses are straight by measuring between their centers. If the distance is 80mm, they are probably fine. If not, or if they look bent, get them looked at by a bike mechanic because you may have to get new bosses brazed on.

1 Screw in the cable adjuster to reduce the tension on the brake cable. If there is a straddle wire, unhook one end and lift it out of the yoke. On a link wire type of brake, undo the cable clamp with a hex key and pull the cable away from the brake arm.

2 Undo the brake boss bolt, freeing the brake arm and allowing you to pull it off the brake boss bolt. Try to hold the spring and washer in place on the brake boss bolt or they could fly anywhere. Clean up all the parts ready for reassembly.

3 Once you have cleaned and greased the brake bosses, install the spring into the middle hole on the brake boss and reinstall the brake arm followed by the pivot bolt. Turn the adjuster with a wrench until each pad is 2mm from the rim, then lock by tightening the pivot bolt again. It is important to set pads an equal distance from the rim at this point. On standard cantis, you can install the spring in the other holes in the brake boss, if you want to increase or decrease the power of the spring. On V brakes, you must use the middle hole only.

4 To make fine adjustments to the pad-to-rim distance, there is a small screw at the base of the cantilever arm. Adjust by turning the screw clockwise to move the pad away from the rim and counterclockwise to bring the pad closer to the rim.

5 Aim at a situation where the pads are equally spaced, 2mm from the rim. Sometimes the pads are also toed-in about 1mm, but this varies with the type of brake and brake pad. Full brake pad adjustment is covered on page 118.

WHEN YOU NEED TO DO THIS JOB
◆ Brakes feel stiff or jerky when you pull the brake lever and neither lubrication nor a new cable are any help.

TIME
◆ 30 minutes.

DIFFICULTY ⚒⚒⚒
◆ It is sometimes awkward to install the spring in the hole on the brake boss and to adjust pad clearance.

Replacing cantilever cables

Setting up a cantilever brake is all about getting the cable lengths right and centering the brake pads.

Basic cantilever brakes have a short straddle wire, with the ends connected to the two brake arms. The middle section of the straddle wire sits in a channel at the back of the triangular cable carrier. The main brake cable is also connected to the cable carrier, with a normal cable clamp.

To set up a basic cantilever properly, first adjust the length of the straddle wire so that it roughly makes a right angle with the brake arm when lifted in the middle. Fit the straddle wire into the cable carrier next. Then try to gauge where the cable carrier should be fitted on the main brake cable. It must be high enough to pull the brakes on fully, but not so high that it hits the outer cable carrier or anything else that would prevent the brakes working properly.

On both from types of cantilever brake, the main brake cable clamps directly to one of the brake arms, with a short link wire joining the cable carrier to the other one. Early designs have a cable carrier with a bolt running through it, or two separate slots for the cable. The wide slot is for when adjusting the cable, the narrow slot for the rest of the time.

The latest link wire brakes have a cable carrier with a diagonal line running across it, or a round window for the nipple of the link wire.

The first step when fitting a new brake cable is to slot it into the cable carrier. Then slide the flexible hose on to the brake cable and fit the cable into the cable clamp on the brake arm. Adjust the length of the brake cable so that the end of the flexible hose touches both the cable carrier and the brake arm, then tighten the cable clamp. Now hook the link wire into the other brake arm and check that the link wire roughly aligns with the diagonal line running across the cable carrier, as in the picture in step 7.

Next, adjust the spring tension with the small Phillips screws on the brake arms. Spring tension is correct when the cable carrier sits directly below the point where the inner cable emerges from the outer. Now fit the brake pads, but do not worry if they touch the rim at this stage.

Adjust the length of the main brake cable so there is a 2 to 3mm gap between the end of the flexible hose and the brake arm. When you have done so, the link wire should line up with the diagonal line across the cable carrier, as in the bottom picture on Step 7. Provided it does, center the brake pads using the Phillips screws again. Finally, make sure there is at least 20mm free cable above the cable carrier.

On all types of cantilever brakes, the final stage is to adjust the pads properly. This is described on page 118.

Link wire cantilevers

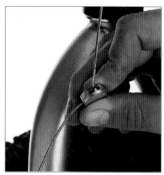

1 Screw in the cable adjuster and pull out the old cable. Check the new nipple fit, grease it lightly, and insert the nipple into the hole. Slide the outer cable over the inner and slot both into the adjuster.

2 On the early type, unhook the link wire from the brake arm next. Then, feed the new brake cable through the wider slot in the cable carrier and slide the flexible hose over the end of the cable.

Straddle wire cantilevers

1 Feed the brake cable into the cable clamp on the cable carrier and tighten lightly. Squeeze the brake pads against the rims and see if you can now lift the straddle cable into the channel on the back of the cable carrier. If it is a tight fit, lengthen the main brake cable slightly. If it is too loose, reduce the length of the cable a little. Tighten the cable clamp.

2 With the brake off, the pads should now sit 2 mm from the rim. If necessary, correct the clearance with the cable adjuster. For top braking power and control, the straddle wire should roughly form a right angle with the brake arm. If it does not, loosen the cable clamp on the brake arm and adjust the length of the straddle wire until it does. Finally, check that there is enough free cable above the cable carrier for the brake to come on fully without fouling the outer cable.

3 Set the length of the brake cable so that the flexible hose touches both the cable carrier and the brake arm. Hook the link wire back into the other brake arm and adjust the spring tension.

4 The spring tension is right when the cable carrier hangs directly below the end of the outer cable. The pads should be an equal distance from the wheel rim. Lengthen the brake cable, if necessary.

5 Finally, check there is enough free cable above the cable carrier to enable the brakes to come on fully. Then move the brake cable into the narrow slot in the cable carrier, the slot for normal braking.

WHICH BRAKE CABLE GOES WHERE?
It is largely a matter of preference. British riders, for example, will route the front brake to the right lever and the left to the rear. Most commonly, however, American bikes use the opposite set up. To avoid confusion it is probably best to route the rear brake through the right lever and the front to the left. When in doubt:

FRONT BRAKE – LEFT, REAR BRAKE – RIGHT.

6 On the later types of link wire cantilever, the cable fits into the brake lever and the cable carrier in roughly the same way. Once you have centered the brake pads with the adjusters, the brake cable must be lengthened to leave a gap of 2 to 3mm between the end of the flexible hose and the brake arm.

CORRECT ANGLE FOR LINK AND STRADDLE WIRES
When setting up any standard cantilever brake, try to get something close to a right angle between the link wire or straddle wire and the brake arm that it is attached to. In order to do this, you will have to experiment by lengthening or shortening the wire or the cable. When set up properly like this, all types of cantilever brakes should feel smooth and powerful.

7 Again on the later types of link wire cantilevers, the wrong angle of the link wire shown in the top picture will cause brake shudder and make it difficult to control the amount of braking. In the bottom picture, the link wire lines up correctly with the diagonal line on the cable carrier. The brakes should work quite nicely.

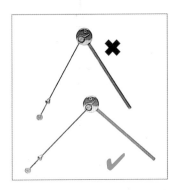

WHEN YOU NEED TO DO THIS JOB
◆ Brakes tend to snatch or lock the wheel.
◆ The cable is frayed or broken.
◆ Lots of effort is needed to make emergency stops, suggesting the cable is sticking somewhere.

TIME
◆ 10 minutes to install a new cable to a straddle wire brake.
◆ 20 minutes for a link wire brake.

DIFFICULTY 🔧🔧🔧🔧
◆ It is easy working on a straddle wire brake, but link wire brakes need careful adjustment to achieve a good balance between stopping power and delicate control.

SPECIAL TOOLS
◆ A cable puller is very useful but not essential.

Side pull brake: strip and adjustment

It should not be necessary to strip down and rebuild side pull brakes very often but if grit gets between the brake arms, it is the only way to get them working smoothly again.

All the moving parts of a side pull brake caliper fit onto the central pivot bolt. This creates a lot of friction, although the nylon washers, brass washers, and even ball bearings sometimes fit between the brake arms help to keep it down. When you strip a caliper, lay all the parts out in order to help you keep track. If you find any washers are damaged or missing, make sure you replace them. They do not have to be an exact fit, so you may be able to use parts from another make or possibly second-hand parts if you find you can not buy new ones.

If you find the brakes tend to stick, it may be possible to increase the spring pressure by reversing both nylon pads where the spring touches the brake arms. Brake levers are often spring-loaded, to make sure that the brakes release as soon as you let go of the brake lever.

You will probably find that the caliper constantly moves to one side, sometimes allowing the brake pad to rub against the rim. If you slip a heavy washer on the pivot bolt so that it sits in between the brake and the fork, you will find it easier to center the brakes and they will stay centered longer.

Campagnolo monoplanar calipers can be stripped in roughly the same way as a standard side pull caliper. Do not strip dual pivot calipers. If they seem to be sticky or notchy, clean the whole caliper in degreaser, paying special attention to the pivots. Then re-lubricate with heavy oil. On some dual pivots, you may be able to increase the spring tension by reversing a nylon pad, because one side pulls.

1 Pull off the cable end cap and undo the cable clamp. Now pull gently on the outer cable—with luck the inner will come out without fraying. Once the cable is free, the nipple may drop out of the cable anchor in the brake lever.

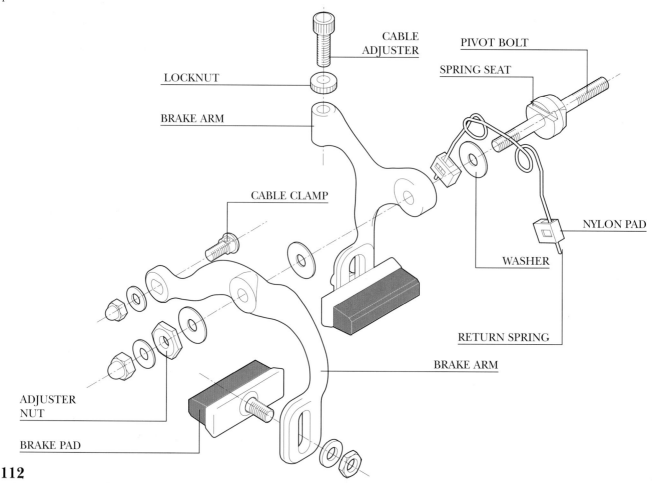

CABLE ADJUSTER

PIVOT BOLT

SPRING SEAT

LOCKNUT

BRAKE ARM

CABLE CLAMP

NYLON PAD

WASHER

RETURN SPRING

BRAKE ARM

ADJUSTER NUT

BRAKE PAD

2 Check how the brake is fixed to the forks next. Sometimes it is a self-locking nut or, more likely, a chromed socket head sleeve bolt. Undo with a wrench or hexagon key, but be careful, it is sometimes hard to get replacements.

3 Pull the brake away from the forks and undo the adjuster nut holding everything in place on the pivot bolt, usually at the front of the caliper. Hook the ends of the spring off the brake arms, then pull the brake arms off.

4 Clean and reassemble, coating all points where friction occurs with anti-seize. Adjust the nuts on the pivot bolt for minimum friction between the arms without any sideways movement. Bolt the caliper back in place.

5 If one of the pads is close to or even touches the rim, loosen the fixing bolt, then use a thin wrench to hold the pivot bolt so that the pads are evenly spaced from the rim. Retighten fixing bolt. You may find this part a bit difficult.

Dual pivot brakes

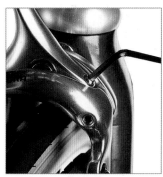

1 Slip the fixing bolt of the caliper into the mounting hole. Then fit the socket head sleeve bolt onto the long end of a hexagon key and screw the sleeve bolt onto the end of the fixing bolt.

2 The end of the fixing bolt will not be visible inside the fork crown, so you will have to waggle the hexagon key a bit until you find the end of the fixing bolt. Then adjust the brake pads for the first time.

3 Fit the wheel back in the frame, centralizing it carefully. Then slacken off the fixing bolt and adjust the position of the caliper so that the gap between the pad and the rim is equal on both sides.

4 Tighten the fixing bolt for the last time and re-adjust the brake pads (see page 118). Finally, use the tiny screw on the rear brake arm to set the pad-to-rim distances exactly equal.

CENTERING A SINGLE PIVOT CALIPER

If you have to keep on centering a caliper, only to find it keeps on moving to one side again, try this trick. Rest the end of a small cold chisel on the circular part of the return spring and hit it sharply with an ball peen hammer. Hit the same side of the return spring as the brake pad that is too close to the rim. This should solve the problem permanently but if you cannot get the knack, go to a bike shop and get it done there.

TOE-IN ON SIDE PULLS AND DUAL PIVOTS

It is nearly always best to install brake pads with about 1mm toe in—see page 118. There is no set way of doing this on a side pull brake, although you can use a crescent wrench to bend the brake arms. But before going that far, try fitting a shaped washer behind the pad holder, as used on MTB brakes and sometimes supplied with new brake pads. You will have to fiddle with the shaped washer until you find exactly the right position for it.

WHEN YOU NEED TO DO THIS JOB

◆ Brake action is still stiff after fitting a new cable.
◆ Braking action feels rough and perhaps sticky.

TIME

◆ Half an hour to strip, clean, and reassemble. Maybe hours to center single-pivot types.

DIFFICULTY 🔧🔧🔧🔧

◆ It can be difficult to refit the return spring and center the brake pads.

New cables for side pull brakes

If you install them carefully and keep them lubed, brake cables will last for years. But if they are frayed or the brakes tend to stick, install new cables now.

Like gear cables, brake cables are now sold in sets or separately. Nearly all pre-packed sets have Teflon-coated wires to reduce friction, with high quality housing. You can also buy separate Teflon-coated inner cables but check the Teflon trademark on the package to make sure.

Brake cables come in 1.5- and 2.0-mm diameter, but both types are much thicker than gear cables. That means you must only use sharp cable cutters – blunt ones will just crush the cable and it will immediately start to fray. Once you have cut the cable to length, fit a cable end cap to prevent unsightly fraying in the future.

Brake housing is also thicker than the type intended for gears. It can be cut to any length and the the same type is used whether it is routed under the handlebar tape, comes out of the top of the brake lever, or goes through the frame.

There are several different shapes of nipple, so take the old cable with you for reference when buying.

If you are considering fitting rubber brake hoods to a road bike, it will save time if you do so at the same time as installing new brake cables.

1 Frayed cables tend to get stuck in the clamp. So cut the cable wherever convenient and extract the remains of the cable with pliers. It will be easier to pull the nipple end out of the brake lever if you slide the housing off first.

6 Spray aerosol lube into the housing until it bubbles out of the other end. Then thread the inner cable into the outer. If it comes out of the top of the brake lever, the housing often sits in a neat separate ferrule.

SPECIAL TOOLS
◆ A cable puller and third tool are desirable but not essential.

DUAL PIVOT BRAKES
Fit new cables to dual pivot brakes using the method given here for ordinary side pull brakes. Use the same type of cable as well, bearing in mind that low-friction cable probably works even better with dual pivots than with side pulls.

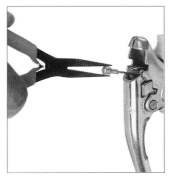

2 In a few cases, you have to peel back the rubber hood and pry out a plastic cover to get at the nipple. If the housing is concealed under the handlebar tape, undo that next, because that will make it easier to install the cable later.

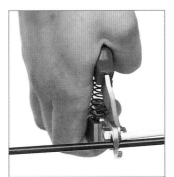

3 Working from the brake end of the housing, try pushing the inner cable out. The nipple should pop out of the brake lever, allowing you to pull the rest out with pliers. If the nipple will not move, lever it out with a screwdriver.

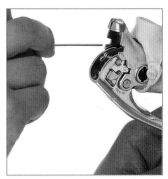

4 If the plastic covering of the housing is cut or damaged, or the cable is kinked, cut a new length of outer and smooth off the cut end if necessary. Use the old housing as a guide to the length of the new one.

5 In concealed cable brake levers, as here, the inner cable passes through a guide hole at the back, emerging by the inner curve of the handlebars. In the older type, the cable simply emerges from the top of the brake lever.

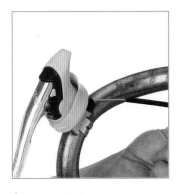

7 Bring the housing up to the brake lever, turn it around the cable anchor until the slot faces you, then slip the inner cable into the cable anchor and seat the nipple. Pull the cables tight and tape the outer to the handlebar.

8 Once the nipple is in place, keep the inner cable under slight tension to prevent it from slipping out again. Pass the inner through the cable adjuster and the cable clamp, then pull it tight. Check that the nipple is still fully seated.

9 Screw the adjuster half way in, then find a wrench to install the cable clamp. Hold the brake pads with one hand and pull the cable tight with the other. Tighten the cable clamp and adjust the pad-to-rim distance, if necessary.

10 Alternatively, tighten the cable clamp a little and use a cable puller to tension the brake cable and pull the brake pads into the rim. Fully tighten the cable clamp, then use the cable adjuster to fine-tune clearance.

WHEN YOU NEED TO DO THIS JOB
- ◆ Brake cable is frayed.
- ◆ Lubing the cable does not free it.

TIME
- ◆ 20 minutes if the cable is routed under the handlebar.
- ◆ 15 minutes if it sprouts out of the top of the brake lever.

DIFFICULTY
- ◆ The only real problem is pulling the new cable tight enough to bring the pads close to the rim. A cable puller helps here.

TWO NIPPLES, ONE CABLE
Brake cables are sometimes supplied with a different nipple at each end. One is a pear-shaped nipple for the hooded brake levers usually fitted with drop handlebars. The other is a drum-shaped nipple for various brake levers fitted to flat handlebars. This includes mountain bikes with cantilever brakes and utility bikes fitted with flat touring handlebars and side pull brakes. You have to cut one of the nipples off before you can use the cable, but make sure the cutters are sharp or it will probably fray immediately.

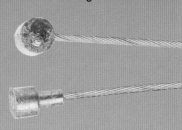

Disc brakes

Even more effective than V brakes, disc brakes are now being installed on mid-price MTBs for the first time. There are many different types, so you should only use this page as a basic guide.

Disc brakes were originally developed for high-performance downhill racing, but are now finding their way onto all sorts of MTBs. The original designs used hydraulic pressure to apply the brakes, but simplified versions using cables are now coming onto the market. Remember that whichever type you use, the discs can only be mounted on special hubs.

Though heavier than cantilevers, disc brakes provide powerful and consistent braking under all conditions. Brakes which work on the wheel rim work best when the rim is clean and dry. In rain or mud, the brake pad tends to slide over the braking surface rather than gripping it. So not only does braking performance fall off badly, you can never be sure just how much it is affected.

Disc brakes, on the other hand, have larger pads that wipe any water or mud off the disc. In addition, the mechanism presses the pad much more firmly against the braking surface.

However, to give instant braking, the gap between the pad and the disc is very small. So small that you should be able to hear a light scraping noise when you spin the wheel. But the small gap also means that when refitting wheels, you cannot just shove the wheel into the frame as usual. You must carefully slide the disc into position between the pads before you install the wheel back in the frame.

The tiny gap between the pad and the disc also makes it vital for the disc to run absolutely straight and true. Do not kick the disc, let it bind on a rock or tree stump, or damage it in any other way. If the disc does go out of true, you will hear it rubbing on the pad and it must be replaced without delay.

As for maintenance, Dia Compe disc brake pads should be replaced every 1,200 to 1,600 miles (2 to 3,000km) or when they have worn down to 6.3 mm in thickness, whichever comes first. Check in your bike handbook or with the seller for other makes. If the pads are not changed when specified, the steel backing will score the disc.

Whenever you install new pads, or if you find that you have to pull the brake lever a long way to stop quickly, you must adjust the gap between the pad and the dis (see the blue box below). The only other maintenance job is to apply a little anti-seize grease to the caliper mounting pins every so often.

Refer immediately to your retailer if the discs get scored or distorted, or if you hear any unusual noises, especially screeching or grinding sounds.

1 To remove a front wheel with a disc brake, turn the quick release lever to the open position. Then let the wheel drop out. If it seems stuck, undo the friction nut a few turns. When refitting, lift it carefully into place and tighten up the quick release again.

5 You can now shake the pad out of the holder, but for health reasons you must not inhale the dust. This means using a light aerosol lubricant to deal with any dust inside the brake body or the pad holder. Check the thickness of the pad to see if it needs replacing.

HYDRAULIC BRAKES (MAGURA)

Just beginning to break into the normal bike market, hydraulic brakes give terrific stopping power, usually at the cost of extra weight. For standard bikes, MTBs, and tandems in particular, hydraulic rim brakes work very well. A hydraulic actuator is installed on each side of the fork and presses a brake pad against the rim. This type of hydraulic brake can be fitted to most bikes. Special frame fittings and special wheels are not required.

Hydraulic disc brakes, on the other hand, can only be installed on suitably-equipped MTB frames. The wheels must also be adapted to cope with the high braking effort involved, with strong, large flange hubs, adapters for the discs, and heavy-duty straight spokes. Two separate hydraulic cylinders are used, with a moving caliper that equalizes the force between the two brake pads. Hydraulic disc brakes cannot be installed on road bikes without major modifications to both the bike and brakes.

Experience so far has shown that although the hydraulic system depends on flexible pipes filled to the brim with hydraulic fluid under pressure, the reliability of both systems is very good. The pipes do not break or burst and you only have to bleed the air out occasionally.

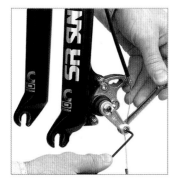

2 To install a new cable, hold the back of the cable clamp with a wrench while you loosen the cable clamp with a hex key. This is also the first step when you have to strip down the caliper to free it or when you want to install new brake pads.

3 As for changing the brake pads, next you have to free the inner pad holder from the caliper body. So locate all three fixing bolts and go around undoing each one, half a turn at a time. This method of working is to prevent any distortion of the parts.

4 When you have removed all three socket-head bolts, gently pry the pad holder away from the disc brake body. The brake pad is held in place with a tiny spring, so pry this away with a small screwdriver. Be very careful because the spring could fly in any direction.

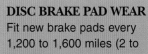

6 Fit the new pads into the pad holder and disc brake body, holding them in place with the springs. However, the springs do not hold the pads in place very firmly and the pins on the pad holder are a tight install in to the holes in the caliper body, so be careful.

7 When properly installed, the pad holder is a snug fit on the face of the disc brake body and there should be an even gap all the way around. Re-install all three hex screws next, tightening them each a quarter or a half turn at a time.

8 The disc brake body sits on three sprung pins. If you press it, the whole assembly should move sideways a little. If it seems to be stuck, strip it down and take care to install it back together again evenly. Finally, re-install the wheel and adjust brake pad clearance.

DISC BRAKE PAD WEAR
Fit new brake pads every 1,200 to 1,600 miles (2 to 3,000km) or when the pad has worn down to a total thickness of less than 6.3mm, whichever comes first.

ADJUSTING BRAKE PADS
Rest the bike on the saddle and handlebars. Locate the adjuster at the fork end of the brake arm. Use a 2.5- mm hexagon key to stop the central bolt from moving while you undo the 8mm lock nut around it about one turn. Turn the hex key clockwise until the pads scrape the disc when you spin the wheel. Turn it half a turn counterclockwise so that the pads scrape the disc very lightly. Hold the central bolt still with the hex key while you tighten the lock nut. Operate the brakes a few times and spin the wheel. There should still be a very light scraping noise. Readjust the pads if the scraping is very loud, or there is complete silence.

WHEN YOU NEED TO DO THIS JOB
◆ Every six months to clean out dust and check pad wear.
◆ You hear squealing or grinding noises when you apply the brakes.

TIME
◆ Half an hour to strip, clean, and re-assemble a disc brake.

DIFFICULTY ✐✐✐✐
◆ Most of the parts are small and are extremely easy to lose. Adjusting the pads can be tricky.

Fitting new brake pads

Safety is the main factor when inspecting or fitting brake pads. Check wear frequently but do not ever let the pads touch the tire—they could wear right through the sidewalls and cause a sudden blow out.

Before changing pads, check the condition of the rims. Light grooves in the braking surface are normal. If the damage is more than about 1mm deep, have your rims replaced immediately because there is a danger of the wheel collapsing. Check the brake pads as well. The chances are that they are not compatible with the rim material (see page 102 for more information). Different pads are required for alloy, steel, ceramic, or carbon rims. And if you install the correct pads, not only will they not damage the rims, they will have more 'bite' as well.

Look also for deposits of pad material on the rims and check if they feel rubbery or slippery. If there is any sign of this, try cleaning the braking surface first with bike degreaser or, if that does not work, methylated spirit. Then scour the rims lightly with an abrasive-backed washing-up pad. This will give the new pads a clean rim to bite on.

Before starting work, check the instructions to see if toe-in is recommended. In some cases, pads are supplied with a special spacer to set toe in. By letting the front of the pad touch first, toe-in takes up the natural spring in the brake arms, preventing chatter and noise when the brakes are used gently.

There may also be a particular way to install the pads. This is sometimes indicated by an arrow which should be fitted so that it points in the direction of rotation of the wheel. But, if the drain slots on the pad are arrow shaped, they should point in the opposite direction. If there is no specific indication, fit the closed end of the pad holder at the front.

Worn cartridge pads have to be removed from the pad holder by undoing a short Phillips screw to release them. The new pads then slip in but do not forget to retighten the screw.

Dual pivot and most center pull brakes are fitted with new pads in the same way as side pulls. But Mafac center pulls have a two-way adjustable fixing similar to the one used on cantilevers. When installing a new brake cable to any center pull brake, use the method given for straddle wire cantilevers.

Standard Cantilevers

1 Slacken off the cable adjustment at the lever and then unhook the link or straddle wire from the brake arm. Loosen the pad clamp by undoing the nut behind the brake arm, holding the pad holder to stop it moving.

WHEN YOU NEED TO DO THIS JOB
◆ Pads are worn down past the wear line or the slots have all worn away.
◆ Pads are contaminated or are causing heavy wear to the braking surface.

TIME
◆ 20 minutes, including alignment of pads and readjustment of cable.

DIFFICULTY ✗✗✗
◆ Not difficult, especially on road bikes.

BEDDING-IN PERIOD
Do not expect your brakes to generate top braking power with brand new pads. The surface of most brake pads is slightly glazed and the braking surface of the wheel rim is never perfectly flat. So allow 20 or 30 miles (35 or 50 km) of gentle riding to bed the new pads in. You can help this process along by applying the brakes lightly when freewheeling downhill.

V

Side pulls

2 Pull the pad holder out of the clamp and check the condition of the pad. If there is a wear ridge either top or bottom, do not misalign the new pad in the same way. Take great care to keep the washers in the right order.

1 On V brakes, the pads are removed in the same way as standard cantis. However, there may be several shaped washers to set the toe-in with. On the other hand, some designs have one shaped washer only (picture top left) to adjust the toe-in.

1 Screw the cable adjuster in and operate the quick release so there is some give in the cable, then undo the brake pad fixing. Sometimes it is a socket head bolt, sometimes a domed nut. Slip the pad out between brake and rim.

2 When fitting a new pad, turn the pad holder to one side if necessary, so you can squeeze it between the caliper and the rim. Leave a gap of about 2mm between the pad and the rim on each side to allow for slightly wavy wheel rims.

BRAKE PAD ADJUSTMENT

Brake pad adjustment must be checked as shown in steps one to three after adjusting the brakes, removing the brake pads, and installing new ones. If brake pads are set parallel to the rim or—even worse —toe-out, it can cause chatter or a squeak when the brakes are applied. On cantilevers, this can be prevented by fiddling with the shaped washers fitted between the brake arm and pad holder.

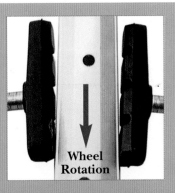

Wheel Rotation

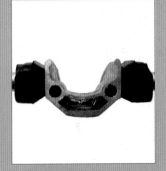

1 Check that the pads are the right way around and tighten the pad securing nut a little. Fit the wedge shaped washer so that there is a 1mm pad-to-rim gap at the front and a 2mm gap at the back. Use a popsicle stick to gauge this.

2 Now pull the brake lever gently and check that the top edge of the brake pad is between 1 and 2mm below the top of the wheel rim. It is permissible to overlap the base of the rim a little, but try to avoid this if at all possible.

3 Next, pull the brake lever again to see if the whole surface of the pad contacts the braking surface. If not, adjust the angle of the pad holder, check steps 1 and 2 again, and tighten up the pad-fixing nut.

RE-SURFACING WORN PADS

When brake pads are fitted incorrectly, a ridge of pad material sometimes forms. This will prevent you from aligning the brake pads correctly with the rim, so cut the ridge off with a sharp utility knife. If that leaves the pad surface very uneven, flatten it off by rubbing the pad surface on medium-grade abrasive paper. Give the pad the same treatment if the surface is greasy or gritty. Do not expect full stopping power until the pads have had a few miles to bed into the rims.

Brake levers

When a brake lever is correctly positioned, you should be able to achieve maximum stopping power, without moving your hands from their normal position on the bars and in full control of the steering.

Mountain bike brake levers all follow roughly the same design. The main difference between budget and quality levers is the provision of reach adjustment and the quality of materials. Do not forget about reach adjustment, as a comfortable hand position on the brake lever helps to prevent you from locking up the brakes on the loose.

Utility road bikes also use a flat style of brake lever with both side pulls and cantilevers. They do not really have enough travel or leverage for side pulls, so make sure you keep the brakes well maintained if your bike has this type of set up.

Racing bike brake levers are all very similar, unless you have STI or Ergopower. On these, the gear change mechanism fills the hood, so the Allen screw fixing is to one side, visible only when you peel back the outside edge of the rubber hood.

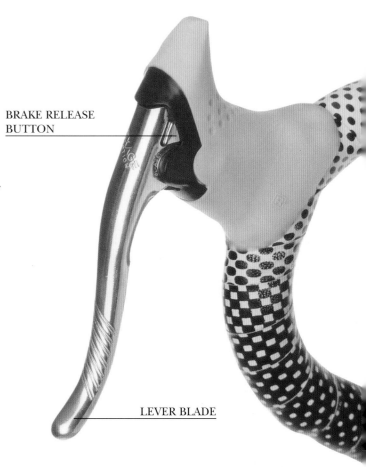

BRAKE RELEASE BUTTON

LEVER BLADE

HANDLEBAR CLAMP BOLT

PIVOT

LEVER BLADE

CABLE ADJUSTER

V BRAKE DANGER

V brakes require special brake levers designed to be used with direct or linear pull brakes. If they are used with brake levers intended for standard cantilevers, the brakes will come on hard almost as soon as you pull the lever and you will find it very difficult to apply the brakes lightly. Servo Wave V brake levers are fitted with an adjuster button on the brake lever, others have a plastic modulator that is only visible when you pull the brake lever. Do not tamper with either type.

Road bikes

1 To reduce the effort needed for braking, lube the brake lever pivot in case it is sticky with old oil. Pull the brake lever next, so you can spray lube on the end of the cable. Work the lever so the lube spreads along it.

2 If the brake lever is loose or you want to adjust its position, remove the cable and, at the back of the hood, you will see the fixing screw. It may do up with a screwdriver, but if you have to use a hex key, go for extra leverage.

3 To remove the brake lever without undoing the handlebar tape, loosen the fixing screw and pull away from the handlebars. On STI levers, pull the edge of the rubber hood back and undo the fixing with a hex key.

COMBINED BRAKE LEVERS AND SHIFTERS ON MTBs
To remove the shifter, take off both cable adjusters and undo the Phillips screws that hold the indicator in place. Pull off and undo the hex socket head screw holding the shifter to the brake lever. To refit, select bottom gear on the shifter and line up the needle with the vertical line, then refit the socket head screw.

MTBs

1 Mountain bike and hybrid brake levers are exposed to the wet, so lube the pivots frequently. Pull the brake lever so that you can lube the cable as well. Give the cable adjuster a squirt of lube so it does not stick or corrode.

2 To adjust position or take off the brake lever, loosen the fixing screw. Where the gear shifter is fitted to the brake lever, the fixing screw is usually tucked under the shifter lever. Push it forward to get at the fixing screw.

3 On quality MTB brake levers, there is a small Phillips screw just behind the cable adjuster. This allows you to alter the reach. Try to adjust it so that you can do an emergency stop using the middle three fingers only.

4 On the other hand, if you have V brakes, you should be able to do an emergency stop using your forefinger and middle finger only. Be careful the first time you do this, as riders have been surprised by the power of these brakes.

WHEN YOU NEED TO DO THIS JOB
◆ Brakes feel heavy, but not gritty, so the cables need lubricating.
◆ The position of your hands when applying the brakes or resting on the brake levers is uncomfortable.

TIME
◆ 2 minutes to lube the levers and cables.
◆ 5 minutes to tighten loose brake levers.
◆15 minutes to remove both levers.

DIFFICULTY ✔✔✔
◆ With racing bike brake levers, it can be difficult to reach the fixing screw at the back of the lever or refit the brake lever to the fixing band on the handlebars.

SPECIAL TOOLS
◆ Long workshop hex keys or T-shaped hex keys are extremely useful when working on road bike brake levers.

CHAPTER 7

WHEELS & TIRES

Most of the time, bike wheels come unscathed through
potholes, punctures, and pile-ups. Nevertheless, they are the most important
and most vulnerable component on any bike, so install the best tires and
wheels you can afford.

Wheel care and inspection

Sooner or later you will have to walk home with a punctured tire or a buckled wheel, but if you use the routine laid down here, that should not happen very often.

Whether you ride on tough mountain bike 'knobbies' or lean-as-a-greyhound road bike wheels, they need very much the same sort of care. Even on budget bikes, the axle bearings should run pretty smoothly. On quality bikes, they should feel as smooth as silk. If they do not, strip and clean the hub bearings immediately or they may be permanently damaged. Nearly all hubs are now fitted with a seal to keep the water out, so once you have the bearings running right, they should be fine for quite a while.

The only regular maintenance hubs need is a few drops of heavy oil. Some have an oil port in the barrel, others have a tiny hole near the axle. But even if there is no oil port, you can always drip some oil around the cones so that it eventually works its way past the seals and into the hub. Take care to clean the area around the axle first, wiping away from the cones, otherwise the fresh oil might carry dirt into the bearings.

Punctures can be a problem, but most can be prevented with a little timely maintenance and a willingness to replace tires before they are absolutely shot.

QUICK
RELEASE
LEVER

VALVE

WHEN YOU NEED TO DO THIS JOB
◆ After every serious ride off road.
◆ Every couple of months on a road bike.
◆ If you ride through a patch of fresh road grit.

TIME
◆ Takes 5 minutes as part of a general inspection.

DIFFICULTY 🔧
◆ Be vigilant on tires.

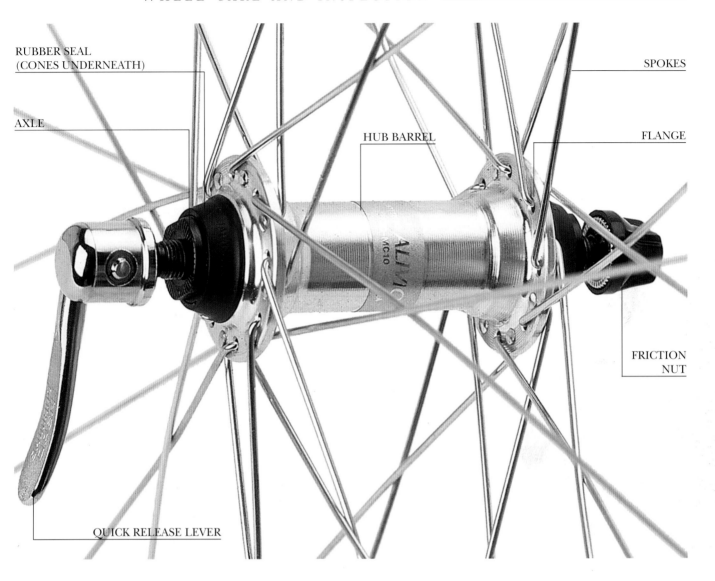

RUBBER SEAL
(CONES UNDERNEATH)

SPOKES

AXLE

HUB BARREL

FLANGE

FRICTION
NUT

QUICK RELEASE LEVER

1 To check a wheel, test the spoke tension first. They should all be roughly the same tension and when you pull two spokes together, they should only move a few millimeters. Now spin the wheel—you can fix slight buckles yourself but loose spokes or bad buckles are best left to a professional.

2 Lift the front wheel off the ground and try to move the rim from side to side. Any movement here suggests that the bearings need adjusting. Next, rotate the wheel slowly with one hand. If you can feel or hear any traces of grittiness in the bearing, the hub needs stripping down and greasing.

3 Even if there is apparently nothing wrong with the hub bearings, you should give them a few drops of heavy oil occasionally. If there is no oil port, spray one side of the hub with aerosol lube to clean it, then lay it flat and squeeze some heavy oil around the edge of the bearing cone.

4 Examine the tire for cuts, gently dig out any flints and flex the sidewalls to check for damage and to make sure the the rubber coating is in good condition. Then spin the wheel slowly to check for bulges in the tread and the sidewalls. Replace any tires that fail these checks or are just badly worn.

Removing wheels

It sounds easy enough to undo the wheels and pull them out but it's the kind of job where you could really use three hands.

When removing or refitting wheels, the first thing to do is operate the quick release on the brakes so there is room for the tire to fit between the brake pads – see page 105. This is particularly important on mountain bikes. Then select top gear so that the chain is running on the smallest sprocket. If you have a workstand, you can remove the wheels with the bike the normal way. If not, or you are fixing it by the roadside, turn the bike upside down.

Quick release hubs are easy to work with but if you do not do them up tight enough, they can come loose and cause an accident. You have to develop an instinct about how hard you have to turn the quick release lever to lock it but if it leaves a mark on your palm when you close it, it is probably tight enough.

Remember that some bikes have a safety device on the forks that prevents the wheel from dropping out even if the quick release lever is not closed. In that case, you have to undo the friction nut several turns before the wheel can be removed.

When re-fitting a wheel with hub nuts, the problem is keeping it centered between the chain stays while doing up the nuts at the same time. Try to steady the axle with one hand and operate the wrench with the other, then swap around, or use two wrenches. For final tightening, use three fingers on the wrench and apply plenty of force.

WHEN YOU NEED TO DO THIS JOB
- ◆ Tire has punctured.
- ◆ Hub bearings need maintenance.
- ◆ Back wheel has pulled over to one side.

TIME
- ◆ 10 seconds to remove and re-install front wheel.
- ◆ 20 seconds to remove a back wheel.
- ◆ 60 seconds to re-install back wheel with nuts.

DIFFICULTY
- ◆ There is a bit of a knack getting the chain on the sprockets and getting it past the rear derailleur.
- ◆ Doing up the back wheel nuts alternately, half a turn at a time each; while keeping the wheel centered, also requires a bit of knack. You may find it easier using a wrench in each hand.

BACK WHEEL SAFETY SYSTEMS

Watch out for the wheel safety retention system on the back wheel of some bikes with hub nuts. One system uses a pear-shaped washer that fits between the hub nut and the drop-out. The tab on the pear-shaped washer has to be fitted into a slot in the fork end, before you fit the hub nut. Both hub nuts are then tightened in the normal way. However, the wheel cannot fall out, even if you have not tightened up the hub nuts enough.

An alternative system is based on dished or conical washers. One washer is fitted under each hub nut, with the serrated side A next to the nuts. A third washer is fitted on the chain side only, between the dropout and the axle. This time the dogged side B sits next to the frame. Tighten the hub nuts in the usual way.

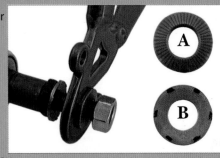

Bolt-in wheels

1 First shift to the smallest sprocket, then undo both hub nuts three or four turns. Good quality hub nuts – usually known as track nuts – have a built-in toothed washer to grip the frame and help prevent the wheel being pulled to one side. Change to this type if your bike only has plain wheel nuts with a separate washer.

2 Pull the rear derailleur backwards so that the chain cage pivots right out of the way. That will allow the wheel to slide forward out of the drop-outs, although it will be tight. Give it a hefty push with your free hand if it sticks.

3 As the wheel drops out of the frame, it will bring the chain with it. So let the rear derailleur return to normal position and try to lift the wheel away. If it will not come, you will have to lift the chain off the sprocket with your fingers.

4 When you're ready to re-install the wheel, pivot the rear derailleur backwards again and pick up the top run of the chain with the top sprocket. Lift the wheel into the mouth of the drop-out, taking care to bring the chain with it.

5 Pull the wheel back into the drop-out and let the rear derailleur spring back. Next, check that the wheel is centered and fit any safety washers. Do the nuts up finger tight, check the rim is centered again, and then tighten the nuts finally.

Quick release wheels

1 Undoing a quick release is a finger and thumb operation. Just hook your thumb around the lever and pull hard outward. As soon as you have overcome the initial locking action, the lever will swing back the rest of the way freely.

2 The wheel may fall out as soon as the quick release is operated. But if there is a safety device on the forks, you will have to hold the friction nut with one hand and turn the lever several times with the other to release it.

3 When re-fitting the wheel, you may have to spread the forks a little to fit the axle into the fork end. Then screw up the friction nut again so that the quick release lever gets hard to move half way towards the closed position.

4 The first movement of the quick release lever requires very little pressure. By halfway, it should need noticeably more force and the final locking stage should take quite a push with your palm. If not, tighten the friction nut a little more.

Tires and tubes

Whether fixing a puncture, changing a tire or replacing a spoke, you will need to remove the tires quickly and without doing any more damage.

RUBBER RIM TAPE

Some riders get a lot of punctures and find great difficulty in repairing them. Others go for months without, so regular puncture sufferers must be doing something wrong. The most common thing is not pumping the tires up hard enough. That makes it easier for flints to cut into the tire, instead of bouncing off. Low tire pressure also causes snakebite punctures when the tube gets nipped between the sharp edge of the wheel rim and the tire. Sometimes this results in two similar punctures on opposite sides of the tube. So keep your tires at the pressure indicated on the side wall, which usually means pumping them up every couple of weeks. That will also helps you to stop wasting energy by distorting the tires every time they touch the ground.

The next cause of punctures is worn tires and tubes. If there are more than half a dozen serious cuts in the tread or the sidewall is deteriorating, fit new tires. Similarly, if a tube is starting to get a network of patches, throw it out. In addition, tread rubber starts to deteriorate after three or four years. So if you are bringing a bike back into use after a while, it is usually worth fitting new tires.

When buying new tires, you can also reduce punctures by paying extra for certain features. Experience has shown that Kevlar reinforced tires really do reduce punctures. Kevlar is a strong composite fiber that is woven into a tape and placed under the tread, although it can be used in tread rubber as well. Both of these applications also extend the life of a tire and so does the silica material now being used in tread rubber.

As for the tubes, butyl ones are best for everyday cycling. They resist punctures, are easy to repair, and reduce the need to pump up the tires. Latex tubes are best for racing because they are much lighter.

If you ever get a puncture on the inside edge of the tube, the rim tape (see the picture above left) is probably damaged or missing altogether, allowing the spoke heads to damage the tube. So check the rim tape every time you take off a tire and fit a new one if it is starting to fray around the valve hole.

Removing the tube

1 Most tubes use a Presta valve. With these, first undo the valve nut with your fingers. Then move to the opposite side of the wheel and push the sidewall away from the rim with your thumb. Insert a tire lever into the gap and pull down.

2 Hook the end of the first lever onto a spoke to hold it there and move around the rim about 4 inches. Push the sidewall back again with your thumb, insert the second tire lever, pull down, and hook the end onto a spoke.

3 Insert the third tire lever in the same way as the other two. You will probably need a bit less force to lift the tire bead over the rim. As you pull the tire lever down, the second tire lever will fall out now that the tire is getting looser.

4 Go right around the tire now, pushing the sidewall away from the rim with your thumbs in case it is stuck. Then unhook one of the tire levers and run it around between rim and tire, lifting the rest of the tire over the rim wall.

5 If using a Speedlever, push the sidewall away from the rim all around the wheel. Then hook the working end under the bead at the base of the sidewall, clip the other end on the axle, and pull it gently but firmly right around the wheel.

6 With one side of the tire now free from the rim, reach inside and start pulling the tube out. When you reach the valve, push the tire bead back over the rim and pull the valve out of the hole. Be careful not to damage the valve.

VALVES AND PUMPS

When working with old bikes, you may come across the Woods tire valve. These have a rubber sleeve which fits tightly around a tube with a hole in one side. When you pump the tire up, the air pressure makes the rubber balloon out slightly, allowing the air to enter the tube. If a bike with these valves seems to have a mystery puncture, the chances are that the rubber gasket has rotted and air is escaping back through the valve. Either fit a new length of valve rubber or fit the modern insert shown here.

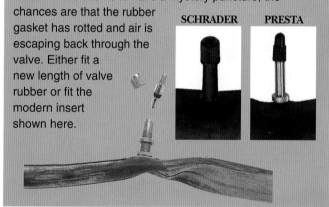

SCHRADER PRESTA

FINDING A PUNCTURE

The easiest way to find a puncture is to pump the tire up before removing it, then listen for the hiss of escaping air. You may be able to see whatever caused the puncture stuck in the tread as well. If this does not work, take the tube out, pump it up a little, and dunk it in a bowl of water or a handy puddle. A stream of bubbles will indicate where the puncture is. But it is only too easy to lose the puncture again when you take the tube out of the water, so wrap the punctured portion of the tube around a finger or mark it somehow.

PREVENTING PUNCTURES

To prevent punctures, install a sealant in the tubes. You connect the bottle to the valve with a short length of tubing and pump some in. The material flows around the tube as the wheel revolves. If a puncture occurs, the escaping air forces some of the material into the hole, where it goes solid and seals the puncture. This does not work on serious gashes, but it seals flint and thorn punctures without any problem. Dispensers for Schrader valves and pre-treated tubes are also available.

Puncture repairs

It is easy to repair a puncture, but you still have to be careful. Keep everything clean and do not expect patches or glue that have been sitting around for years to work properly.

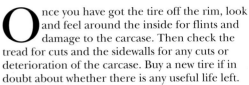

Once you have got the tire off the rim, look and feel around the inside for flints and damage to the carcase. Then check the tread for cuts and the sidewalls for any cuts or deterioration of the carcase. Buy a new tire if in doubt about whether there is any useful life left.

Most cyclists on a long run or a serious cross country ride carry a spare tube and some even carry a spare folding tire. These have flexible beads, usually made of Kevlar, and will fit in a bottle cage or under the saddle.

Riders sometimes have trouble pumping up a tire with a Presta valve, using a push-on adaptor. The main point is to slacken off the valve nut two–thirds of the way first, and then push in the valve stalk for a second, just in case it is stuck. Push the adaptor evenly onto the valve and hold the pump horizontal. Finally, wrap your index finger around the valve to steady the pump in the correct position.

Repairing punctures

1 Even if you spot the puncture easily, it is easy to lose sight of it. So draw a circle around the spot with the yellow crayon found in most puncture outfits. Do not mark the actual area of the puncture.

2 Lightly roughen the area around the puncture with abrasive paper, again supplied in most puncture outfits. This makes a key for the adhesive and removes any dirt or rubber dust from the surface.

3 When you are satisfied that the tube is clean and dry, select a suitable patch. Apply a thin, even coat of rubber solution around the puncture, then put the tube somewhere out of the wind to dry.

4 If you are using standard rubber patches, wait until the rubber solution is dry. Then lift a corner of the white backing with your finger nail, pull the rest off, and press the patch into position.

Refitting the tire and tube

3 Make sure the tube is sitting inside the rim and settle the tire on the rim evenly all the way around. Starting at the valve, push the tire over the edge of the rim with your thumbs.

1 Rotate the wheel to position the valve hole at the top and lift the sidewall so that you can insert the valve in the hole in the rim. Do not screw on the valve nut yet, but do keep the valve at right angles to the rim.

2 Work your way around the wheel, tucking the tube into the deepest part of the rim. Try to avoid twisting or creasing it as you do so. This is usually easier if you pump the tube up a little.

TIRE CHOICE

When a tire is taking a beating, the casing will start to bulge, indicating that puncture resistance is getting low. New tires are needed without delay but there is an enormous variety to choose from. Puncture resistance is covered on page 128. But as for wear, tires with silica in the tread not only last longer, they are also faster for a given energy input, especially the dual tread compound, two colour type. On MTBs that are in daily use on the road, the full knobbly is no fun. It is hard work and best kept for serious off-road work. That leaves the multi-purpose tire capable of mild cross country work but with reasonable road performance, or the semi-slick, available right down to a width of 1.5in, with very little tread. Top road tires also have dual compound silica-filled treads with a Kevlar layer but there is not much point in going narrower than 700 x 23 as that sacrifices both comfort and performance.

TOP: Semi-slick tire for road use and commuting on a mountain bike.
MIDDLE: A full-out cross country tire with a Kevlar casing. Foldable.
BOTTOM: Directional multi-purpose tire. Good for the mud but also OK on the road.

5 Try to position the center of the patch right on top of the puncture and smooth it out from there to avoid trapping any air. Then use the end of a tire lever to press the patch down, especially the edges.

6 With feather-edge patches, you also wait for the rubber solution to dry. Pull off the silver foil backing next, position the patch on top of the puncture, and press down from the center with a tire lever.

7 After 20 seconds, fold the patch in half. The cover should then split, allowing you to peel it off from the center. Feather-edge patches blend into the tube and the edges shouldn't lift at all.

8 When using glueless patches, you still have to prepare the area with abrasive paper. Then remove the backing and apply the patch, but think of them as a get-you-home product, not permanent.

4 Continue this process all around the tire, pulling the other side of the tire in with your fingers and forcing the tire wall over the rim with your thumbs. Try to avoid using the tire levers at all.

5 If you use a tire lever, don't trap the tube against the rim or you'll puncture the tube again. Pump the tire up a little to straighten out the tube, check that the valve is upright, and screw on the valve nut.

Strip down hubs

Water, dirt, and grit are the things that stop hub bearings running smoothly. So check them over occasionally and strip and re-grease when they start to feel rough.

You have probably decided to strip the hubs down because of problems revealed during one of your occasional inspections. But if you've been out in a downpour, especially when riding across country, it's always worth checking the hub bearings in the next few days. In addition, serious off-roaders should reckon on a routine strip down every three months or so, although road riders can stretch that to a couple of years if the wheels keep running smoothly.

Most hubs have some sort of rubber seal to keep out the wet stuff but they only work up to a point. So don't ever point a hose at the hubs, let alone a pressure washer, no matter how dirty your bike.

Some seals are external to the hub and fit around the axle, locknut and cone, pressing on the flange of the hub. More often, the seal is set in the flange itself and presses on the outside edge of the cone. In this case, it may be necessary to carefully pry the seal out in order to get at the ball bearings. This second type can be backed up with additional seals made by various accessory manufacturers. These seals are designed for mountain bikes but there is no reason why they cannot be fitted to other types.

A front hub is shown in the picture below to keep things simple but rear hubs come apart in more or less the same way.

1 Remove the quick release skewer by holding the friction nut and twisting the q/r lever until it comes to the end of the thread. Watch for the conical springs on the skewer, each side of the hub.

2 On mountain bikes, there is sometimes a separate rubber seal around the cones which helps to prevent water entering the hub bearings—they just pull off. But internal seals are more common.

5 When you have removed the cone and locknut on one side of the axle, you can pull the axle out the other side. Be careful, as some of the ball bearings might come with it and drop onto the floor.

6 Almost certainly some ball bearings will be left in the hub, stuck there in the grease. Dig them out with a small screwdriver or a pen top and scrape out as much of the old grease as you can.

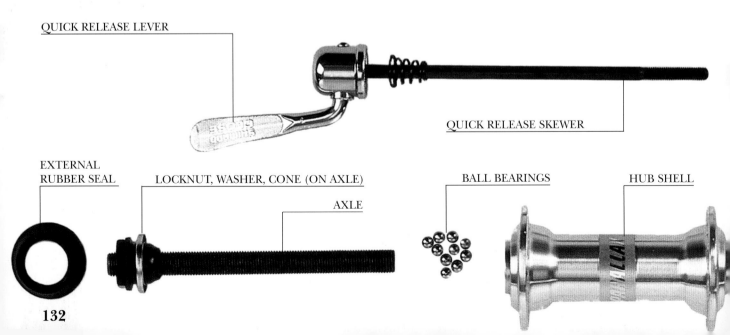

QUICK RELEASE LEVER

QUICK RELEASE SKEWER

EXTERNAL RUBBER SEAL

LOCKNUT, WASHER, CONE (ON AXLE)

AXLE

BALL BEARINGS

HUB SHELL

3 Use a cone wrench to hold the axle while you undo one of the locknuts. It will take quite a lot of force to start with. If you are working on the back wheel, it is usually best to work on the non-chain side.

4 Undo the lock nut and pull off the lock washer. This sometimes has a tag which fits into a groove in the axle, so you may have to pry it off with a screwdriver. Finally, undo the cone itself.

WHEN YOU NEED TO DO THIS JOB
◆ When the bearings feel rough or seem to drag a bit when you turn the axle with your fingers.
◆ During a big overhaul.

TIME
◆ 5 minutes to remove the axle.

DIFFICULTY
◆ This is the easy part, provided that you have a proper cone wrench.

SPECIAL TOOLS
◆ At least one cone wrench, preferably a pair of them.

GREASE FOR HUB BEARINGS
That tin of ordinary grease in the shed is probably lithium-based grease for cars. Do not use it on your bike because it has three big drawbacks. One is that it is too heavy, so it causes a lot of drag in the bearings. Two is that it soon ceases to work if water gets in. Three is that it can thicken up badly and so lose most of its lubricating properties. Use grease specially formulated for bike bearings instead. It is thinner, tolerates water better, and does not thicken up as much. Up to this point, nobody has come up with a miracle grease for bikes, so any reputable bike grease is fine for packing the bearings in hubs, pedals, and headsets.

100 gms
WELDTITE
03004

CONE

LOCKNUT

LOCK WASHER

SPRING   FRICTION NUT

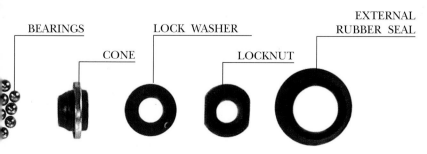

BEARINGS   LOCK WASHER   EXTERNAL RUBBER SEAL

CONE   LOCKNUT

Grease and adjust hubs

If hubs need cleaning and fresh grease, go through all the steps here. If they run smoothly but the bearings are loose, go through the adjustment procedure only.

The first thing to do after stripping the hubs down is check the cones for damage. If there is any problem at all, it's best to fit new ones. Check also that the axle is straight – if one or other end of the axle appears to move up and down when you roll it along a flat surface, fit a new axle too. Most cones have the same thread and shape, so there is usually no problem finding new ones but if you are dealing with budget hubs, you may have to buy a complete new axle.

The core part of this job is adjusting the cones so that they apply the right amount of pressure to the bearings. Aim for the point where you cannot feel any movement at all on the axle but it still turns without any feeling of dragging or grittiness.

Finding this exact point is mostly a process of trial and error and even professionals do not expect to hit it first time, so do not worry if you also have to re-adjust the cones a few times.

The problem is that when you finally tighten the locknut, it increases the pressure on the cones and through them on the bearings. So to get the cone adjustment right, you have to leave just enough slack to make up for this.

When you think you have got the adjustment right and the axle turns really smoothly, pop the wheel back into the bike and see if you can detect any movement at the wheel rim. The distance of the rim from the hub magnifies any slack, so it is OK if you can detect a tiny amount of movement. Re-check the adjustment after your next ride.

If the rim is not buckled but nevertheless rubs on the brake blocks somewhere, the cones probably need tightening a fraction.

THEY ARE THE PITS
Once you've stripped the hub bearings down, the next step is to inspect the inner surface of the cones for damage and wear. The cone above left is a new, high-quality item, which is the ideal. The middle one is pitted and should not be re-used at any price. The right-hand cone has some wear, which will probably accelerate from now on. Re-use to stay mobile only, while you track down a new one.

1 Clean away all traces of old lubricant, and coat both bearing tracks with a thin layer of waterproof grease. Do not be tempted to fill the barrel of the hub with grease or it will be forced out later and make a horrible mess.

4 If you are re-using the old cones, screw the loose one onto the axle and tighten it down until there is just a little play left in the bearings. Spin the wheel slowly—it should already turn much more smoothly than before.

5 If you are fitting new cones, adjust their position on the axle so that the axle is central in the hub. Fit the lockwashers and locknuts and screw them down onto the cones. Do not leave out the washers or it will be harder to adjust the cones.

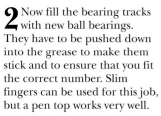

2 Now fill the bearing tracks with new ball bearings. They have to be pushed down into the grease to make them stick and to ensure that you fit the correct number. Slim fingers can be used for this job, but a pen top works very well.

3 Now spread a little more grease on top of the bearings. If the old cones are fine, there is no need to undo the one still in place on the axle. But you must clean everything up carefully before inserting the axle in the hub.

WHEN YOU NEED TO DO THIS JOB
◆ During an inspection, you've found that the hub bearings are not very smooth or there is movement at the rim.
◆ As part of a major overhaul.

TIME
◆ 40 minutes, including stripping down and degreasing.

DIFFICULTY
◆ Provided you have got proper cone wrenches, the only real problem is adjusting the cones just right. Do not forget that the grease is quite thick to start with, so the bearings will loosen up a bit later.

SPECIAL TOOLS
◆ You really need two cone wrenches. These are long wrenches, slim enough to fit the narrow flats on the cones and locknuts. But remember, if you use too much force, the jaws will distort and become almost useless.

6 If you are re-using the old cones, the axle should already be centered and the locknut fully tightenend. But when fitting new cones, check the position of the axle and then tighten the locknut hard against the cone on one side.

7 Turning to the other cone, screw it in or out until there is a tiny amount of play left, then tighten the locknut against the cone. If you judge it right, this final tightening will eliminate that last little bit of movement in the axle.

Wheel truing and spoke replacement

Do not be afraid to tweak the spokes a little if your wheels are out of true but this is really a job for a professional.

If a wheel has very loose spokes and is seriously out of shape, your local bike shop will sell you a replacement. They will probably offer you a choice of standard machine-built wheels or hand-built to your own specification. If you decide on a hand-built wheel, it can be carefully tailored to suit your weight, your style of cycling, and so on.

Spokes are held into the wheel rim by square-sided nipples, which are tightened or loosened with a spoke wrench. However, the square end is tiny so you must use a tightly-fitting spoke wrench. If you use a poorly-fitting wrench, you will round off all the nipples and the wheel will have to be rebuilt.

Occasionally, you will find that the nipples have seized and will not move. Try loosening them off with spray lube. If that does not work, the wheel will have to be rebuilt.

Any time that you tighten a nipple, the end of the spoke pokes a little further through the rim and could puncture the tube. To prevent this, file the spoke end flush with the nipple.

When replacing spokes, the crucial thing is to follow the pattern exactly, crossing the same number of spokes and alternating sides where they fit into the hub.

Truing a wheel is a matter of increasing the spoke tension on one side to pull the rim straight and slackening it on the opposite side to make up for this. Treat each bend separately and work from the edges to the middle, a quarter turn at a time at the edges and half a turn in the middle.

Fitting a new spoke

1 Spokes usually break just below the nipple or near the bend close to the hub. It is normally easy to extract the remains, but if the spoke has broken on the chain side of the back wheel, you will have to remove the sprockets.

2 Thread the new spoke into the empty spoke hole and wiggle it around so that the head seats nicely. Look at the previous spoke to see if the new spoke goes over or under the spoke that it crosses and follow this pattern.

Truing a lightly buckled wheel

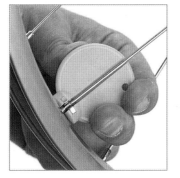

1 Unless you are doing a roadside repair, it's best to take off the tire and tube first. Then fit the wheel in the frame and spin it slowly, noting where and how bad the bends are.

2 If the rim bends to the left, loosen the left-hand spokes a little and tighten the opposite, right-hand ones. Work from the ends of the bend towards the middle. True each bend before moving on.

3 Do not try to get it right all at once but work little by little, checking that you are doing it right by spinning the wheel frequently. When the wheel is true, stress relieves the spokes to settle them in place.

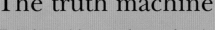

The truth machine

It is okay to tighten up a loose spoke or iron out a slight bend in the rim for yourself. However, all the spokes in a wheel should be kept at a high but even tension and once you have slackened off some and tightened up others, you may have weakened the wheel quite considerably. The answer is to let a bike mechanic true up your wheels as soon as they start leaving the straight and narrow. Professionals use a special jig which allows them to correct side-to-side and also up-and-down bends. They will also re-tension the spokes so that the wheel stays true longer.

WHEN YOU NEED TO DO THIS JOB:
◆ As a roadside repair.
◆ When the wheel wanders a bit but you don't have the time to take it to a bike shop.

TIME:
◆ 20 minutes to true a slightly wavy wheel.
◆ 30 minutes to remove a tire and fit a new spoke.

DIFFICULTY: 🔧🔧🔧🔧
◆ Quite difficult because you have to balance loosening and tightening spokes. Take it slowly and check frequently that you are reducing the buckle, not making it worse.

SPECIAL TOOLS
Spoke wrench. The most common spoke sizes are 14, 15, and 16 but check before you buy. Do not use a combination spoke wrench because they are difficult to use and likely to damage the nipples.

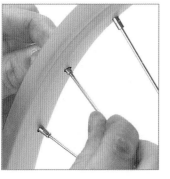

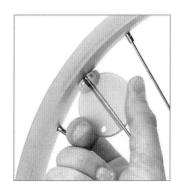

3 Remove the rim tape and pull out the rest of the old spoke. Unscrew the nipple on the new spoke and bend it gently so that you can thread the end into the spoke hole. Check that the spoke head is still seated correctly.

4 Do the nipple up finger tight and check that the new spoke is following exactly the same route as the previous one. If the rim has angled seats, make sure you tighten the nipple right down into the base of the insert.

5 Twang the spokes with your fingers to get an idea of how tight they are. Then progressively tighten the new spoke until it is under the same tension as the rest. File off the end of the spoke, if necessary, and true up the wheel.

BARS & SADDLES

When on a bike, most of your weight is taken by your hands and rear end, although your feet should take some as well. For maximum comfort, position your handlebars and saddle so that the weight falls equally on them both.

Component check

The handlebars, stem, and saddle take a lot of weight between them, so check occasionally that they are not deteriorating with age and that all the bolts are tight.

Rust and corrosion on iron and steel are easy to spot. But it seldom becomes a problem for cyclists because steel frames and components have plenty of strength in reserve. It is possible to envisage a frame becoming fatally weakened by rust, but it seldom happens in practice.

Aluminum alloy also corrodes, but it is hard to spot because the white flecks of oxide blend in with the silver color of the metal. However, in normal conditions, corrosion stops at the surface. Handlebar stems and seat posts are a very tight fit in the frame and so here aluminum and steel come into close contact. If water gets into this area, it forms an electrical connection between the two metals and corrosion can then move very fast.

You can combat this effect by using anti-seize grease wherever different metals come into contact. But even if you do so, it is worth occasionally checking highly stressed alloy components like seat posts and stems. If you do find serious pitting or even minor cracks on the surface of the aluminum, replace without delay.

The welding on alloy frames and components can also fail, although most of these are now put together using automated Tungsten Inert Gas welding. In this process, the area being welded is surrounded by inert gas, so the molten metal cannot be attacked by the air. Nevertheless, it is still worth taking an occasional look at the welds, particularly when the items are more than three years old.

1 One problem that can affect the seat post is corrosion inside the frame. Next is the saddle clamp cutting into the seat post. Third is overtightening of the seat post clamp or saddle clamp. Replace if necessary.

2 Occasionally check that the seat post clamp is tight, but do not overtighten. If you do, that could cause cracking if the seat post clamp is a separate component, or distortion if it is part of the frame.

3 Handlebars can crack close to the stem in heavy use, so consider installing handlebars with a built-in brace. But keep an eye on the mounting bolts and handlebar clamp bolts as they are also highly stressed.

4 With threadless headsets, tightness of the stem clamp bolts must be checked occasionally. On triple-clamp forks, the socket head bolts holding the legs into each clamp also need attention.

5 Traditional style stems only need a check on the main bolt, which must be tight enough to stop the handlebars from moving in the frame. On all types of stem, check that they line up with the front wheel.

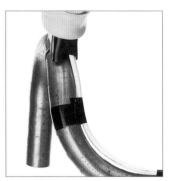

6 Handlebars are made from very thin gauge tubing. If the brake lever band starts to cut into the metal, cracks may fan out from that point. Check whenever you remove the handlebar tape, just in case.

Take care not to overtighten the stem cap.

7 As welded stems get older, it is possible for corrosion to get a hold in the welds themselves. Occasionally check the weld bead and surrounding metal for pin holes and cracks and replace if necessary.

SAFETY LIMIT LINE

When setting up your riding position or adjusting the height of the saddle or handlebars, you must check that the limit mark is not visible. If the handlebar stem or seat post are pulled out so far that the limit marks are visible, there is a strong possibility that they will either fall out of the frame, or break due to the additional stress placed on them.

If you need to set the saddle higher than permitted, install a longer seat post than standard. But now that there are many new ways of building a frame, you must be very careful that the new seat post is exactly the correct diameter for the frame.

You cannot do the same thing with the stem but you may be able to solve the problem by installing a different style of handlebar. For example, replacing straight handlebars with risers.

Handlebars and stems

Although they come in many shapes and sizes, nearly all handlebars and stems go together and fit on a bike in the same way.

Between the front forks and the stem, but normally out of sight, is the steerer tube. At the bottom end, the steerer tube is permanently joined to the forks while the handlebar stem is connected to the top end. Traditional stems are held into the steerer tube by means of an expander bolt. This screws into a cone which is drawn up inside the stem, causing it to expand and lock in position inside the frame. More often, the expander bolt screws into a wedge which locks against the wall of the steerer, with the same effect.

You change the height of the handlebars by undoing the expander bolt. If the handlebars will not move after you have dislodged the wedge, squirt some light lubricant around the bottom of the stem and wait. After a while, try holding the front wheel between your knees and twisting them vigorously from side to side as you lift. You can alter the angle of the handlebars just by loosening the clamp bolt.

The alternative way of attaching the stem to the steerer tube is to clamp it to the outside. This system also uses an unthreaded headset and the stem presses down on the top steering bearing to hold the fork and bearings in place. The Aheadset/Tioga version of this system uses a disc held in place with a socket head bolt to close off the top of the stem, as arrowed in the large picture on page 141. Other versions, as shown in step 5, have a plain top.

When you have finished working on the stem or handlebars, always re-check that the bolts are tight enough and that the stem lines up exactly with the front wheel.

Removing the handlebar stem

1 On some traditional stems, the top is closed off with a large rubber plug. Pull out the plug and look for the socket headed bolt a little way below. Do not confuse this type with the Aheadset type. On these there is a much smaller socket head bolt on top of the stem.

2 This socket head bolt is sometimes buried so deep that you will only reach it with the long end of a hex key. Slip a narrow piece of tubing over the short end of the hex key so that you will have enough leverage to undo the expander bolt.

Adjusting handlebars

1 To change the handlebars, start by removing the brake levers, gear levers, light brackets, and so on. But do not bother if you are only altering the angle of the bars, just remember to adjust the position of the levers as well.

2 Now undo the handlebar clamp. You only need to loosen it a few turns to adjust the position of the bars, but remove the bolt completely if you are separating bars from the stem. In a few cases, the clamp has two smaller bolts.

SAFETY LIMIT MARK
When adjusting the handlebars, do not pull the stem out so far that the limit mark becomes visible. The mark is sometimes faint, so check the lower part of the stem very carefully.

MIXING AND MATCHING
In a perfect world, every make of handlebar would fit every make of stem. Unfortunately, although handlebars are identical in principle, different makers work to different sizes. So you may have to open up the handlebar clamp or accept heavy scratching when installing or removing them. If you do have to open up the clamp, be very careful because it is only too easy to crack the metal if you use excess force.

3 On older versions of the expander bolt stem, there is no rubber plug. In this case, it is much easier to undo the bolt with a hex key or spanner. Once you have undone it about four turns, give the head of the expander a sharp blow with a medium hammer.

4 If that does not dislodge the expander bolt, cushion it with a piece of wood and hit it harder. The stem itself may then be stuck in the steerer tube. Apply light lube to the bottom of the stem and tap the top of the stem with your hammer to help loosen it off.

5 Some stems that clamp on to the outside of the steerer tube can be removed by just slackening off the clamp bolts and lifting. You can adjust the height of the stem by varying the number of washers beneath, but for safety reasons, do not use more than four.

WHEN YOU NEED TO DO THIS JOB
◆ After installing a new saddle or changing its position.
◆ If you are not comfortable.

TIME
◆ 30 minutes to install new handlebars.
◆ 5 minutes to reposition stem or handlebars.

DIFFICULTY ⚒⚒⚒⚒
◆ It can be quite difficult to remove the handlebars without scratching.

3 You can now try to work the handlebars out of the clamp. Be careful, there may be a separate metal sleeve around the handlebars, inside the clamp. Do not hurry because it is only too easy to scratch the bars badly, especially drops.

4 If it is impossible to pull the handlebars out of the stem, try refitting the clamp bolt the opposite way around with a coin in the slot. As you tighten the bolt, it will open up the clamp, but this trick only works when the bolt hole is threaded.

ADJUSTABLE STEMS
Some hybrid bikes now come with an adjustable stem and it is worth considering one if you are having trouble getting a comfortable riding position. To alter the angle of the stem, loosen the clamp bolt that holds the stem to the steerer tube. Next, undo the socket head bolt on top of the stem until it is quite loose, lift the handlebar assembly and re-tighten the top bolt. Then re-tighten the clamp bolt in front of the stem, making sure that it is exactly in line with the front wheel. Remember that raising the handlebars also brings them closer to you. The type of stem shown

here only works with a threadless headset but there are versions that work with most types of bikes, including racers, though some do look a little strange.

Grips and tape

Nothing ages a bike more than a tattered set of handgrips or torn and dirty handlebar tape. Luckily, replacements cost very little.

Nearly all mountain bikes are sold with flat handlebars or risers. To make sure they fit most people, manufacturers sometimes fit them too wide for the majority of riders. This is OK on short journeys, but it forces many riders to use a tiring spread-arm riding position. If you are installing new grips, consider whether you would be more comfortable with narrower handlebars or with bar ends that give you an alternative hand position.

The simplest way to reduce the width of the bars is to cut a couple of inches off the ends. But before you do this, check that it will leave enough room for the bar ends, brake levers, and shifters. If you decide to go ahead, plumber's pipe cutters will do the job very neatly. You can get these at any Wal-mart, but buy good ones—the cheap types are a pain. Do not remove more than a couple of inches of handlebar on each side, otherwise it might be difficult to retain full control of the steering.

There are many different types and styles of bar end but the cheaper ones made of aluminum alloy suit most riders. When you are installing them, do not overtighten the fixing bolt or the aluminum tube may collapse under the pressure.

You do not have to use rubber grips on a mountain bike. Handlebar tape, as used on nearly all road bikes, is fine. This is available in various materials and lots of different colors and patterns. The most popular type is slightly padded plastic, but you can get cork, which gives a cool sweat-free grip, and cloth. Cloth ages fast, but always feels good. When you reach the brake levers with the tape, mold the tape neatly around the clamp and the hood.

Top-quality racing bike handlebars have a groove for the brake cables. Use a few short lengths of tape to fix the brake cable in the groove before you apply the main covering.

BAR END CLAMPS

Bar ends come in only one size and should fit any normal handlebar. But if you have problems getting the clamp onto the handlebars, try filing a slight chamfer on the end of the bar and lightly greasing the inside of the clamp. If that does not work, it may be possible to open up the clamp with a screwdriver. But do not use any more force than that, otherwise you could crack the clamp and that is potentially very dangerous.

New grips for flat bars

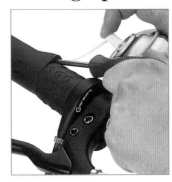

1 If the old grips are finished, just cut them off. If you want to re-use them, open up the grip with a screwdriver, fire some spray lube into the gap and pull them off.

2 You will probably have to twist and pull the grips at the same time to drag them off. Underneath, the bar will be covered in sticky goo, so wipe it clean with a cloth.

Taping drop handlebars

1 Pull out the handlebar end plugs first. Some have a central screw which must be loosened first to ease off the pressure, but most just pull out or pry out with a screwdriver.

2 Undo all the old tape, cutting it with a utility knife if necessary. Then roll back the rubber brake hood and use a short length of tape to cover the edge of the lever.

Installing bar ends

1 If you are keeping the same handgrips, lightly tap the end with a large hammer to cut through the rubber. Once you have cut through in places, finish the job with a knife.

2 Then check that you have removed enough of the rubber grip to get the full width of the clamp onto the handlebar. Smooth off the end of the handlebar with a file.

3 Gently push the bar end onto the end of the handlebar. If necessary, cushion the clamp with a piece of wood and tap lightly until the full width of the clamp is on.

4 Sit on the saddle and adjust the angle of the bar end. Then tighten the clamp bolt but do not overdo it. Apply some clear glue to the safety plug and push it all the way in.

3 Remove the rest of the goo with methylated spirit, then spray the grip area with standard hair spray. Slide the new or re-used grip on before the hair spray dries.

4 If you do not have any hairspray, try aerosol paint. Use the palm of your hand to push the grip along the handlebar but move fast or it will stick in the wrong place.

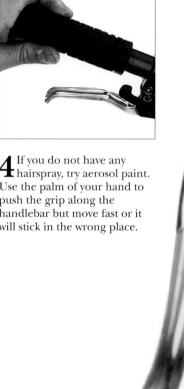

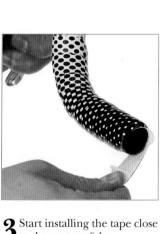

3 Start installing the tape close to the center of the handlebars, overlapping it carefully and stretching it around the brake levers. When you get to the end, tuck it in neatly.

4 Fit new bar end plugs as a final touch. Sometimes they go in easily, but you may have to use the palm of your hand to screw them around and around until they fit flush.

WHEN YOU NEED TO DO THIS JOB
◆ Grips and tape are old and tatty.
◆ Handlebars are too wide for comfort.
◆ You want to install bar ends to give a better riding position when climbing hills.

TIME
◆ 15 minutes to install new grips.
◆ 30 minutes to cut down handlebars with pipe cutter and adjust the position of the brake levers.
◆ 15 minutes to remove old handlebar tape and install new.

DIFFICULTY
◆ Pretty easy, even if you decide to reduce the width of the handlebar.

SPECIAL TOOLS
◆ Plumber's pipe cutter.

Saddles with clamp fixing

Although simple to look at, saddle clips are very difficult to install back onto a saddle once you have taken them off.

There is seldom any need to separate a saddle clamp from the saddle, but if you have to do so for some reason, re-assemble all the bits in the correct order on the through bolt. Then hold the assembly together by tightening both nuts an equal amount. This keeps the through bolt in the center of the clamp. Do the nuts up finger tight only.

Position the saddle rail retainers face outward and slip them onto the saddle rails from the rear. Then slacken one of the nuts off a little and rotate the curved outer retainer so that it closes off the saddle rail retainer. Repeat the process on the other side and tighten both nuts.

With the clamp fitted to the saddle, push it onto the slimmer section of the seatpost, then tighten both nuts equally.

Install the circular part of the saddle clamp above the point where the thin section of the seatpost bulges out to the main part. Otherwise it will eventually weaken the metal so much that the saddle falls off.

To allow you to adjust the riding position, the saddle slides backward and forward on the rails. You can also change the angle of the saddle. This is best done by undoing both nuts a little at a time until they are loose enough to allow the ridges on the outer retainers and the saddle rail retainers to jump over each other. Retighten the nuts as soon as you have completed the adjustment.

SADDLE

SADDLE RAILS

SADDLE CLAMP

SEAT POST

SEAT POST CLAMP

SEAT POST HEIGHT
Most seat posts are marked with a line showing the minimum length which should be inside the frame at any time. To put it another way, you should never see the line on the seat post when the bike is in use. As a rule of thumb, at least one third of the seat post length must stay inside the frame.

Final saddle adjustment

1 It is very important to get the angle of the saddle right, otherwise too much of your weight will rest on the most sensitive part of your anatomy. Undo the nut on one side of the saddle clamp first.

2 Do not undo the nuts too far or it will be impossible to make fine adjustments to the saddle angle. To tilt the nose downward, lean on the front of the saddle and lift the back with your hand.

3 A saddle clamp also allows adjustment backward and forward. Loosen the nut slightly on one side and thump the back of the saddle with the heel of your hand to move it forward and vice versa.

LEATHER SADDLES
Solid leather saddles must be allowed to dry out naturally, whenever they get wet. If the rain soaks right into the saddle, apply a dressing to feed the leather and build up water resistance. Tighten the nose bolt if the leather sags – the makers supply a special spanner.

Altering saddle height

1 Saddle height is adjusted by undoing the saddle clamp bolt until it is fairly loose. But the seatpost should be a tight fit in the frame, so it will not move easily. Turn it from side to side to get it to move, then coat the seatpost with copper-based anti-seize grease to prevent future problems.

2 Turn the saddle 2 or 3in each way and lean on it to adjust downward. To raise the saddle, move it from side to side and lift at the same time. Then tighten the saddle clamp bolt fairly hard.

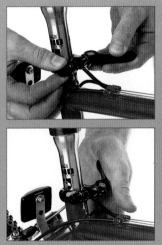

SEAT POST BINDER
Lots of mountain bikes have a seat post binder instead of a bolt. They are similar to the quick release on a hub so, when you tighten the binder, it must take a definite effort to lock it. If it does not, tighten the nut on the other side from the lever. Once you get used to whipping the seat post in and out, you can use it as a security device. Taking the saddle off also makes it easier to load your bike in a car.

WHEN YOU NEED TO DO THIS JOB
◆ Installing a saddle to a standard seatpost, usually on an older type of bike.
◆ Swapping a saddle from a new bike to an old one.
◆ Adjusting the riding position.

TIME
◆ Installing a saddle clamp could take 5 minutes or drive you mad and take 15 minutes.
◆ Adjusting saddle height is easy, unless the seatpost is stuck in the frame.

DIFFICULTY ✗✗✗✗
◆ Refitting a saddle clamp is one of those jobs where you need three hands—one to hold the clamp, one to hold the saddle, and the other to use the spanner. It is best to assemble the clamp away from the saddle and install it back all in one piece. If that doesn't work, get a bike mechanic to sort things out. Spray light lube or penetrating oil around the base of the seatpost if it seems to be stuck in the frame.

Saddles with micro-adjustable seatpost

Seatposts with a built-in clamp are neat and light, but some have more fore-and-aft adjustment than others.

Seatposts with a built-in clamp are far superior to those with a separate one. They look better, weigh less, and are not so awkward. Most have a good range of adjustment but this varies between different types and makes. So if you are unusually tall or short, you may have to change your seatpost to get the correct riding position. Take a look at the 'layback' design (pictured below) if you want to get the saddle well back over the back wheel.

There are many variations on the basic design, some of which are not micro-adjusting because there may be 2 or 3mm difference between each possible saddle position. Maybe a problem for the perfectionist, but not most riders. Other types have a two-bolt 'see-saw' design where you undo one bolt and tighten the other to adjust the saddle angle.

There are two important dimensions to watch – diameter and length. Diameter is critical because there are at least fourteen sizes you could come across. These vary between 25.4mm and 31.8mm, so the differences in diameter are very small. Nevertheless, if you try to install the wrong seatpost, it will either seize in place and make the frame useless, or it will be too loose to ever tighten properly.

So when buying, either take the old seatpost or, better yet, the frame with you. Get the bike shop to check the correct size with calipers or a micrometer before buying.

Most road bikes have a seatpost 220mm long, most MTBs use a 300mm length because of the smaller frame sizes. But provided the diameter is correct, you can use an MTB length seatpost in a road frame, cutting it to length if necessary. BMX bikes have a steel seatpost, 400mm long.

CREAKING NOISES
It is quite common for a saddle to make creaking noises, most often when you're climbing a hill or sprinting. If this annoys you, try a light coat of anti-seize grease on the clamp bolt as well as the cradle and clamp. Do not be tempted to overtighten the alloy clamp bolt because it will easily snap.

WHEN YOU NEED TO DO THIS JOB
◆ When installing a new saddle or seatpost.
◆ To adjust your riding position.

TIME
◆ 10 minutes to install a new saddle or seatpost.
◆ 2 minutes to make a change to the saddle position.

DIFFICULTY 🔧🔧
◆ You should find it much easier with a micro-adjustable seatpost than working on one with a separate clamp, whether you're installing a new seatpost or adjusting the position of the saddle.

Installing saddle

   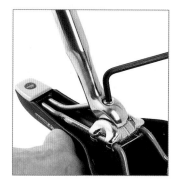

1 On the standard design single-bolt seatpost, the saddle clamp is held in place by a bolt through the cradle. In the type shown, the cradle is part of the seatpost, but it's usually separate. Always use anti-seize on the clamp bolt.

2 Fitting the saddle is usually easier if you take the seatpost out of the frame. Turn the saddle upside down, support the top part of cradle with two fingers, and lay the square nut under the cut-out portion, supported by your fingers.

3 Now lay the other part of the cradle on the saddle rails. Then lower the saddle and clamp onto a firm surface and check that the cut-outs in both parts of the cradle line up with the square nut. Do not worry about saddle position.

4 Finally, fit the clamp bolt through the hole in the seatpost, through both parts of the clamp, and screw it into the square nut. Then tighten the clamp bolt until the cradle grips the rails, allowing you to remove your fingers at last.

Adjusting saddle

  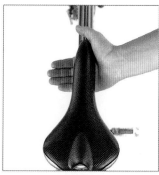 

1 When getting a new bike ready for the road or bringing an old one back into action, coat the bottom of the seatpost with anti-seize grease to prevent corrosion. Then set the saddle height using the guide lines on page 10.

2 For fore-and-aft adjustment, undo the clamp bolt one turn. But to adjust the angle, hold the cradle together with one hand while you undo the clamp bolt several turns. Lift and rock the saddle to change the angle and tighten.

3 Do not try to slide the saddle to a new position because there is too much friction in the cradle for you to do that accurately. Tap it with the palm of your hand instead, moving it by only a couple of millimeters or so at a time.

4 When you are satisfied with the new saddle position, check that the clamp bolt is tight (not overtight) and that the saddle is exactly aligned with the frame. Finally, do a short test ride to make sure you are comfortable.

SUSPENSION SEATPOSTS

For extra comfort, consider a shock post. They fit in the same way as a standard seatpost but have about 2in of up-and-down movement to absorb bumps. The hex key adjuster allows you to alter the spring tension or install a stronger spring if necessary.

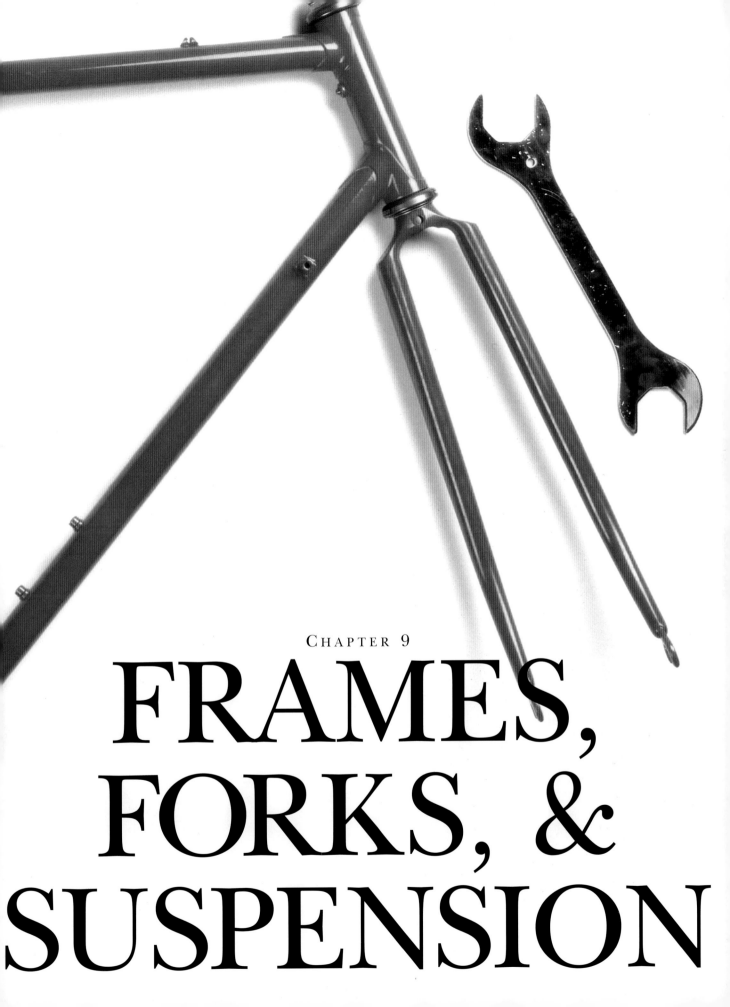

CHAPTER 9

FRAMES, FORKS, & SUSPENSION

Frame materials and design

Fully-assembled bikes are such a good value that it is seldom worth buying a separate frame and building it up yourself, unless you need a custom frame or want the fun of designing your own bike.

Exotic materials like carbon fiber and titanium are found on big-budget frames. But when you are talking sensible money, steel and aluminum frames offer fantastic all-around performance whether you want a bike for mountain biking, touring, and sports riding on the road, or road racing.

The best-known makers of tube sets are Reynolds of Britain, who make steel tubes, and Columbus of Italy. They mainly use steel but also make the Altec aluminum tube set. However, most aluminum tubes are known by numbers.

The Japanese firm Tange supplies high-grade Prestige and other tube sets to many American and Taiwanese bike builders but does not have a clear range structure. These makers also use True Temper tube sets made in America. Unfortunately, the label Cro-Mo on its own only tells you that it is a very basic tube set. 4130 cro-mo is one step up from that, the cheapest sort of hardened tubing. To sum up, you tend to get what you pay for from all the big mountain bike makers and standards are surprisingly high.

Apart from full suspension MTBs, most bike frames are all based on triangles, which concentrate the stresses where one tube is joined to the next. So quality frame tubing is drawn thicker at the ends where the stresses build up and thinner in the middle, to save weight. The thick ends are called butts and the tubes are spoken of as single butted if only one end is thicker and double butted if both ends are manufactured like this. Nearly all quality tube sets are double butted but some high quality sets are triple butted, with a stronger section of tubing in the middle.

Apart from the tubing, the other factors in frame quality are the methods that are used to join the tubes together and workmanship.

Lugs are the traditional way of joining steel tubes. The gap between tube and lug is filled with molten brass to hold everything in place. The only thing that can go wrong is that if the tubing is accidentally overheated, it can become weak or brittle. However, the latest air hardening steel tubing becomes stronger if it is heated and then allowed to cool slowly in the air. Do not buy a frame with quality tubing and clumsy lugs.

Welded steel and aluminum tubes are usually joined together using Tungsten Inert Gas (TIG) welding. This process is automated and can produce consistently high-quality lightweight frames in very large numbers. In TIG and similar processes, the welding head is surrounded with inert gas to cool the weld and prevent the molten metal being attacked by oxygen from the atmosphere. The welding machine should produce an even bead of weld with a regular pattern of overlapping ridges. Do not buy a frame if the bead looks clumsy or is pinholed.

Utility Bikes

Utility bikes are built from heavy carbon-steel tubing. Male and female cruiser bikes are now replacing the traditional sit-up-and-beg style, but the whole bike still leans backwards for a relaxed riding position.

Mountain Bikes

Many full suspension mountain bikes use variations of the Y-frame design. This design makes it easy to arrange the rear suspension but is only economic because the deep oval frame members can now be TIG-welded.

1 On TIG welded frames, there is usually a bead of welding in the angle between each tube. If the ripples in the weld are regular, the bead thickness is even, and there are no pinholes at all, the welding should be pretty reliable.

2 Some welded frames are much better finished. The welds are so carefully sanded that one tube appears to blend seamlessly into the next. Traditionally-built fillet brazed and silver soldered frames have a similar seamless quality.

3 Composite—usually carbon fiber—frames have this same seamless appearance. The joints are often reinforced with webs or gussets. You can tell they are not metal because the tubes do not ring when you flick them with your finger.

4 Any reasonable-quality MTB frame should have two sets of bottle mounts and a well-thought-out set of cable eyes along the top tube. There should also be a built-in gear hanger and the front derailleur cable should pull from the top.

5 Built-in derailleur hangers indicate that you are looking at a reasonable quality road bike frame. A chain peg (top arrow) is also a nice feature but most top quality frames now have short vertical dropouts, not long horizontal ones.

6 Most high quality road and MTB aluminum frames are fitted with keyhole seat stays and curved chain stays. The bend in the seat stays allow them to bend a little, giving some much-needed resilience to an aluminum frame.

7 Road frames are often fitted with aerodynamically-shaped straight fork blades. They may be made of aluminum, but carbon fiber is said to be more comfortable because the 'give' in the forks can be very closely controlled.

8 Touring frames need more braze-ons than any other type. There should be rack-mounting eyes at the top of the chainstays, on the rear drop outs, and on the forks. Chain stay pump pegs leave more room for bottle bosses.

Racing Bikes

More and more quality racing bikes are built with aluminum tubes. The frame angles are upright to position the rider for top pedaling efficiency and agility, with short, straight forks for quick steering.

Touring Bikes

Traditional touring bikes are built with 531 steel tubing and look like racing bikes with fenders. But now an MTB influence is creeping in with the use of V brakes, MTB gears, and multi-position handlebars.

Frame inspection and crash repair

Bike frames are strong but a crash can kink the tubes or put the whole thing out of kilter. You will not always be able to spot the damage, but a quick check after a crash is a sensible precaution.

Luckily, most bike frames have plenty of reserve strength, but it is not unknown for them to go out of alignment. When this happens, the wheels lie at different angles to each other and the bike will not steer straight.

Sometimes you will be able to spot this by eye, especially if you check the frame from different directions. Comparing the appearance from the front and the back also helps. If you suspect that the alignment is out, have the frame checked professionally and, if necessary, realigned.

Watch out also for damage to the forks, which take the brunt of many minor crashes. Luckily, it is now quite easy to find replacement forks for road bikes. As for suspension forks, you will probably have to strip them and get a professional to assess the damage.

Most frames have brazed-on fittings. If you have trouble getting the rear derailleur mounting bolt or the gear lever screw to enter the thread, have the threads cleaned out with a tap by a professional bike mechanic. This is most likely to happen to the rear derailleur hanger because it has a coarse thread.

Frames built of aluminum do not behave in quite the same way as steel frames. It is the welds that are most likely to go on an aluminum frame, especially ones with large diameter, oversize tubes. Alloy frames also age more quickly than steel, so inspect them occasionally for cracks in the welds and pinholes.

FRAME TUBING QUALITY

REYNOLDS
500 – Non-butted chrome molybdenum tubes for mass produced bikes.
525 – Butted cro-mo (chrome molybdenum alloy steel) tubing, for brazed frames with lugs and for TIG welding.
531 – Famous since 1935. Alloyed with manganese so no high temperatures. TIG welding is out. Tube sets now available for racing (531C) and touring (531ST).
725 – A cro-mo butted tubeset for TIG welding and brazing, with lugs and without. Much stronger than 525.
631 – Air hardening so gets stronger as it cools after TIG welding or brazing. As strong as aluminum, weight for weight.
853 – Also air hardening, as strong as titanium.

COLUMBUS
Aelle – Heavy, budget priced cro-mo.
Gara – Still a budget product but butted.
SL and SLX – Roughly equivalent to 531.
Thron – Quality tubes for mass production.
Brain – High quality with internal reinforcement.
Neuron – Top quality and very expensive.
Columbus Altec – Drawn from 7005 aluminum, alloyed with zinc and magnesium.

ALUMINUM ALLOY TUBE SETS
Easton – Supplies quality aluminum tubes.
5000 – Alloyed with magnesium and easy to extrude, so good for components like handlebars. Also used for frames.
7005 – Probably the most popular aluminum frame material. Has a reputation for high performance budget bikes. Easy to weld.
T4, T6 etc – Indicates that the component has had a specific heat treatment.

Checking for crash damage

1 Position yourself at the front of the bike and look along the frame. You should be able to see if the short head tube and the seat tube that carries the saddle line up.

2 Stand over the bike looking down. You will be able to see if the horizontal top tube lines up with the diagonal down tube. Check also that the forks splay out an equal amount.

3 Now look along the frame from the back. The rear derailleur should hang straight down and the seat tube should align with the head tube. Check also that the seat stays are straight.

4 Most importantly, run your fingers down the back and front of the forks, checking for ripples in the tubing. Next, take a look to make sure that the fork curves smoothly. Then take the front wheel out, so you can see if it fits back in easily and is centered exactly between the fork blades.

5 Finally, run your fingers along the underside of all the tubes, because damage such as the tiny ripples in the tubes arrowed in the picture on the right very easily go unnoticed during a purely visual inspection. Luckily, the sense of touch will often pick up defects that the eyes just skate over.

Neither the tubes nor the welds have cracked on the crashed frame in the picture, showing the amazing strength of a really well-built frame.

WHEN YOU NEED TO DO THIS JOB
◆ When buying second-hand.
◆ After a crash.
◆ If you feel the bike is not running straight.

TIME
◆ 10 minutes is enough for a thorough inspection from several different angles. Always try to look along the frame against the light.

DIFFICULTY 🔧🔧🔧
◆ When you first start, you will think you're going cross-eyed, but you will soon get the hang of it.

Suspension set up

Full suspension bikes and hardtails with suspension forks only need proper setting up to get anything like the best out of them. Your height, weight, and riding style all affect how they work.

When setting up a suspension bike, you have to adjust the force needed to compress the springs. The idea is that when you put your weight on the saddle, the springs should sink down or sag by about 30% of their total travel. This does not refer to the length of the springs themselves, but the distance the forks or the rear suspension move between the unloaded and the fully loaded position.

If the forks or rear suspension reach the end of their travel when riding over rough ground, this is known as bottoming out. It should be avoided because it tends to shake your eyeballs out and can damage your bike, including the suspension itself. Bottoming out can also occur if the front of the bike pitches up or bounces off the ground. Then the other end of the spring travel is reached, which is known as rebound. The 30% of spring travel allocated to sag is intended to keep down the amount of bottoming out. If it happens a lot, that is a sure sign that your bike is not properly set up.

Stick to 30% sag if you are setting up a hybrid with suspension forks or a hardtail MTB with front suspension only.

When adjusting any kind of forks, try to adjust both legs evenly. If there is a difference between the springing of the legs, it will tend to produce uneven wear and possibly lead to distortion.

Many of the cheaper suspension forks and full suspension bikes have steel coil springs only. They do not have any sort of damping, so the bike tends to bob up and down because there is nothing to control the springs or absorb the energy of the bumps.

When riding a suspension bike, try to develop a smooth pedaling style to stop the bike from bobbing around. And on hills, change down to the lower gears early so that you do not have to get out of the saddle. This will keep the back wheel glued to the ground, not hanging in mid-air where it cannot transmit any pedal power.

FULL SUSPENSION FRAME DESIGN
There are two main types of rear suspension:

URT stands for Unified Rear Triangle. In this design, the bottom bracket is part of the rear triangle itself. Therefore, the main frame pivot has to be placed in front of the bottom bracket. This eliminates any variation in chain length and the frame can be made lighter, which is particularly important on cross country bikes.

The other type, Active Suspension, is generally more complicated and expensive than URT. The simple version is triangulated. The single swing arm type uses motor bike technology. And linkage suspension is based on a rocker and push rods, so it is related to race car technology.

Front suspension

1 To set up the suspension, you must know what the total travel is. This figure is in the handbook but if that has been lost, choose one point on the top, fixed part of the forks and another on the lower part that moves relative to the rest of the bike. Measure the distance between them. Once you have that figure, ask a friend to hold the handlebars while you sit on the saddle and check that the riding position is okay.

2 Bounce up and down to settle the suspension. Then measure the distance between the two chosen points and take that away from the first figure. That gives you a figure for the amount of sag when you sit on the bike. Now work out what percentage the second figure is of the first.

3 The amount of sag should be around 25 to 30% of total fork travel. If less than 25%, the forks are too stiff, so turn the adjuster counterclockwise one turn. Turn the adjuster the other way if sag is over 30%. Repeat steps 1 and 2 until the sag amount is correct.

Rear suspension

1 Rear suspension is adjusted by turning the spring seat on the suspension unit; there is no dial adjuster. If sag is less that 30%, turn the spring seat counterclockwise to increase it and clockwise to decrease it. Keep adjusting the spring seat until you get 30% sag.

2 If you are unusually heavy or light, adjusting just the spring seat may not work. You may be able to change the unit to another mounting point to increase the spring travel but this might make the ride too bouncy. Or you may be able to install a different spring.

3 It will take a bit of trial and error to get the sag right. When you have, sit on the saddle and check that the bike stays level. If not, try to strike a compromise between 30% sag and a level bike. And be ready to adjust further as you learn how a full suspension bike works.

REAR SUSPENSION PIVOT

When buying a full suspension bike, check that the pivots are large and meaty looking. They should also have some kind of built-in protection against water but you should still keep the area free of dust and mud. In theory no maintenance is needed but a squirt of aerosol lube does no harm.

Suspension fork overhaul

Suspension forks must not be neglected. Inspect the protective rubber boots regularly and be prepared to strip and regrease the forks several times a year.

Crashing up and down over rough ground, suspension forks take more of a beating than any other component on a bike. What is more, unless the sliding parts are protected by good condition boots, dirt will get between the moving parts and cause rapid wear. So day to day, keep an eye on the boots and do not ride cross country if they are defective.

Every couple of months, the forks must be stripped so you can check the bushings and regrease the stanchions. The bushings are plastic tubes that fit in the tops of the fork legs. The fork stanchions are a close fit in the bushes, so they can slide up and down smoothly, without any chatter.

If the bushings are regreased frequently, the stanchions will slide more smoothly and wear on the plastic bushing will be kept to a minimum. However, depending on how fast you ride and the terrain, the bushings will have to be replaced sooner or later.

You only apply a fairly thin smear of grease to the bushings, spring or elastomer stack, and upper stanchions. But you must use a synthetic type because mineral grease will attack the rubber parts. RST recommends Sylkolene Pro RG2, available from their dealers but other fully synthetic greases will do.

Upgrade kits are available for some forks, offering better quality boots and bushings. Soft rubber boots will always outlast hard plastic ones, but the bottom end of the gaiter must be held in place with a cable tie to stop dirt getting in.

You can usually get alternative springs to help you set up the suspension and you can change elastomers too. Cream ones are hard and blue ones soft. But fit the same stack of elastomers in each fork leg to avoid problems. The elastomers themselves damp down movement pretty well, but plenty of bikes are sold with spring forks and no damping. Consider upgrading to forks with oil or air damping if you find the front of the bike bobs around a lot or tends to act like a pogo stick.

Sprung forks

1 Before starting the actual strip down, degrease the forks with solvent and water and dry them off. Then undo the countersunk Phillips screws or bolts holding the fork brace to the fork legs.

2 Check the brake pivots next to see if they are bent or cracked. Then unscrew them using a wrench at the base of the pivot to avoid slippage. Lift the fork brace out of the way.

Triple clamp forks

1 Strip the forks off the frame and degrease the whole fork assembly including the steerer tube and any rubber components. Then undo the top caps with the special wrench supplied.

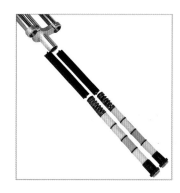

2 Once you have undone the top caps, withdraw the complete elastomer stack and wipe off any grease. Check that none of the elastomers are damaged in any way.

3 Lift the wheel end of the forks and undo the socket head bolt buried in the end of each fork leg. You can then pull the lower legs off the stanchions and degrease them inside.

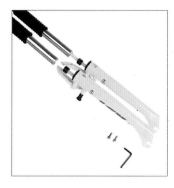

4 With the forks stripped and degreased, carefully inspect the plastic bushings at the top of the lower legs. If some areas of the bushing look shiny or scored, they need changing.

5 During a major overhaul, pull the compression rod out of the stanchions, degrease, and inspect for damage. Finally, reassemble by reversing the previous procedure.

3 Pull back the rubber gaiter and grasp the steerer tube with one hand. With the other, turn the lower leg counterclockwise and pull it right off. Use channel locks cushioned with rag to start it moving if necessary.

4 Wipe away any excess grease and unscrew the spring using long-nose pliers. Use your thumbs to push off the bush around the top of the fork legs, then clean and degrease this area as well.

5 Degrease inside the fork leg and all the bits. Place the new bush on a hard surface, sit the lip of the fork leg on the seal, and lean on it with all your weight. Grease the springs and lower legs, then reassemble.

Standard headset

Stripping and greasing a headset is easy but fitting a new one requires special tools. It is a job for the bike shop, not for you.

When a bike is past its first youth, you may find the steering is not as smooth as it was. This could be because the headset needs a strip down and clean.

On the other hand, it is possible that the headset needs changing. That is because every time you go over a bump, the bearing race on top of the forks lifts and smashes the ball bearings into the bottom ball race. In the same way, the top bearing race lifts away from the bearings, so they do not get as badly battered. When this has happened tens of thousands of times, depressions are formed in the bottom races which the ball bearings have to climb in and out of when you turn the steering. This makes the steering feel stiff and notchy, and can only be put right by fitting a new headset.

If you ride a bike with the headset loose, it increases the force with which the ball bearings smash into the races and speeds up the formation of pits. So if the front brakes start shuddering or the steering feels shaky, check for play in the headset and adjust immediately. Otherwise the headset will deteriorate fast.

TOP BEARING RACE

LOCK NUT

LOCK WASHER

HEAD TUBE

BOTTOM BEARING CUP

FORK RACE

FORK

1 When stripping and greasing a headset, you may be able to get away with lifting the handlebars out of the frame and letting them hang there. But it is easier to remove the forks if you take off the brake levers and shifters.

2 Your first move is to undo the lock nut. A tight-fitting wrench is best, but a pair of channel locks or a big crescent will do. Most quality bikes have a soft alloy headset which you will damage if you do not use a well-fitting wrench.

3 Below the lock nut is the spacer washer. In some cases, the steerer tube has a flat on one side and there is a matching flat on the spacer. If the bike is fitted with center pull or cantilever brakes, the brake cable hanger also fits in here.

4 Unscrew the top race next. If the bike is standing on the floor, the steerer tube will not move. But if you have a workstand, the forks will drop out as you undo the top race. Take care the ball bearings do not drop all over the floor.

5 Gather up the ball bearings. Some will probably be stuck in the top cup, others on top of the forks. Clean everything up with solvent and inspect all four bearing tracks for signs of wear, particularly the bottom bearing cup and fork race.

6 Stick new ball bearings in the top and bottom cups with waterproof grease. Do not use caged bearings. Fit the fork back in the frame and screw it down the top race to hold it there. Then adjust the top race to eliminate any play.

7 Fit the lockwasher and screw the lock nut down on it. Now apply the front brake and see if you can feel any movement. If you cannot detect any this way, try wedging your finger between bottom race and fork crown.

8 Check there is no friction at the handlebars and no movement in the bearing. When it is right, hold the top race with one wrench and tighten the lock nut against it with the other. Test ride and re-adjust as necessary.

O-RINGS AND SEALS

Watch out for very thin rubber O-rings in grooves around the bearing cups. These are very effective at keeping water out but must not be stretched or broken or you will find it impossible to refit them. Off-road and touring bikes should be fitted with external seals available at bike shops.

WHEN YOU NEED TO DO THIS JOB

◆ The bike is in for a general overhaul.
◆ There is a chatter when you turn a sharp corner or apply the brakes hard.
◆ Turning the handlebars requires effort or the steering is not smooth and accurate.

TIME

◆ 30 minutes if you just lift the handlebars.
◆ 40 minutes if you decide to remove the brake levers and shifters.

DIFFICULTY 🔧🔧🔧

◆ It is not too difficult to strip down, grease and adjust a headset, especially if you've got suitable wrenches. Do not try fitting a complete new headset because it requires special tools to press the bearing cups into the frame accurately.

SPECIAL TOOLS

◆ Headset wrenches.

Aheadset and Tioga headsets

These days, most mountain bikes and high-end road bikes are fitted with a stem, headset, and forks designed as a single set of components to save weight.

The components of a standard headset are held together by the pressure of the top bearing race, which is threaded and screws onto the steerer tube. Aheadset and similar systems are held together by the handlebar stem, which is clamped onto the steerer tube with bolts. Neither the top race nor the steerer tube are threaded, so you cannot interchange the two designs.

On the Aheadset-type, you control the free play in the steering by increasing or decreasing the pressure of the stem on the top bearing race. To adjust the bearings on an Aheadset, undo the clamp bolt and tighten or loosen the socket head screw on top of the stem until there is no play in the steering, but it turns with a minimum amount of effort. Re-tighten the clamp bolt and check adjustment by applying the front brake and seeing if there is any movement detectable at the top of the forks.

On other designs you do not have to undo the socket head bolt, you just undo the clamp bolts and apply pressure to the top of the stem with your hand,

The only real drawback of this system is that it is impossible to adjust the handlebar height more than about half an inch . For more adjustment, you have to install a stem with more or less lift.

Cartridge bearings are now creeping into use, but do not alter the way the headset is fitted or adjusted.

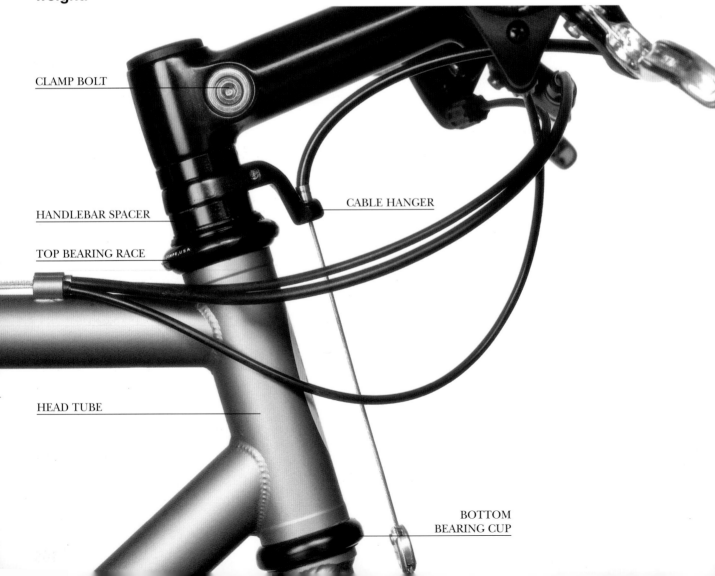

CLAMP BOLT

CABLE HANGER

HANDLEBAR SPACER

TOP BEARING RACE

HEAD TUBE

BOTTOM BEARING CUP

1 The top cap is held in place with a socket head bolt which screws into a special nut inside the steerer tube. The caps are designed to break if you overtighten the bolt, so do not fit non-standard ones.

2 Lift the cap off the stem. Check it has the same brand name as the stem, and not the name of an accessory maker. If you look down the stem, you will see the special nut inside the steerer tube.

3 Undo the clamp bolt holding the stem to the steerer tube. Sometimes there is just one, others have a pair, but the latest design has a single clamp bolt buried in the front of the stem.

4 Once you have removed the clamp bolt, you can lift the stem off the steerer tube. Be careful as there is now nothing holding the fork into the frame and it could fall out if you do not hold it in place.

5 Take off any spacer washers or the brake cable hanger, which may sit under the stem. Locate the conical washer that locks the top bearing race to the steerer tube in some types. Pry it out and lift off.

6 The top bearing race is now free, so raise the front of the bike, allowing the forks to drop. Ask a helper to hold the forks while you check the bottom bearing cup and fork race for wear and pitting.

7 Reassemble by reversing steps 1-6. Coat with anti-seize and check that the stem moves up and down freely. Adjust the steering bearing with the socket head bolt and cap. Tighten up the clamp bolts.

WHEN YOU NEED TO DO THIS JOB
◆ During a major overhaul.
◆ If the steering is stiff.
◆ When the forks seem to chatter in the frame.

TIME
◆ 30 minutes. This type of headset is simpler to work on, so you probably will not need to take the brake levers and shifters off.

DIFFICULTY
◆ The hardest thing about this job is grasping how it is all held together.

Clamp-on stem

1 If there is any play in the steering bearings, undo the bolts that clamp the stem to the steerer tube. Check that it moves up and down smoothly, without sticking at any point on the steerer tube.

2 On triple clamp forks, undo the bolt holding the top clamp to the steerer tube. Check that the clamp is not binding. It must move freely so that you can press the stem and clamp onto the top steering bearing.

3 Check that the stem moves up and down freely. Then adjust the steering bearing by pressing on the top of the stem and then tightening the bearing clamp.

TIOGA HEADSETS
Tioga headsets are very similar in principle to the headsets shown here. However, they usually have a circlip, a circular spring device that fits in a groove, to hold the forks in the frame. Before you can remove the top bearing race, you have to remove the circlip by prying it off with a screwdriver or a pair of circlip pliers.

CHAPTER 10

BIKE
EXTRAS

Bikes do a hundred different jobs but they will do most of them better with some carefully selected additions. Just be careful you do not turn your lightweight rig into a tank.

Make yourself visible

The majority of new bikes do not have any provision for lights. But a certain amount of preparation will turn any bike into a perfectly safe 24-hour machine.

Legally, if you plan to use your bike after sundown, it must be equipped with one white front light and at bare minimum, a rear reflector. A bright rear light, however, is a good idea, even if most localities in the United States don't require it. You only need to see a bike with a flashing light to realize how well they work, even when the street is saturated with light.

Flashing lights do not have a conventional bulb. Instead, the light is generated electronically by means of a Light Emitting Diode (LED). These are vastly more efficient than a bulb with a filament, so although they are tiny, the batteries have a long life. LED lights usually have a switch with three positions—off, steady, and flashing.

Battery-powered lights are the cheapest way of complying with local laws, and in conjunction with high-power halogen bulbs, they are quite bright until the batteries start to fade. Unfortunately, they fade fast and regular night riders often use rechargeable batteries to get around this problem. Batteries last longer with standard tungsten bulbs but are nowhere near as bright.

Various forms of dynamo use the rider's own energy to power the lighting. The commonest variety runs off the side of the tire but there is an argument that the roller tends to slip. To prevent this from happening, some dynamos are mounted under the bottom bracket. In this position, it is possible to install a much larger, slip-resistant roller.

Maybe the best solution for regular winter bike riders is the rechargeable battery which fits in a bottle cage. The lights are connected to this battery with electrical wire. When the lights dim, or as part of a weekly routine, you recharge the battery as you would a car battery.

New batteries and bulbs

1 LED lights usually have a switch at the back, plus a clip for fixing the light to your clothing.

2 LED lights have a close-fitting plastic case. To install new batteries, locate the notch where the red lens meets the black casing. Place the tip of a screwdriver in the notch and pry the case apart. Take care not to damage the rubber seal.

THE HIGHWAY CODE
The 1999 edition of the Highway Code has a lot more helpful advice for cyclists and cycling than the previous one. So get a copy to bring yourself up to date, especially about cycle lanes and the areas being created in front of the other traffic for cyclists at busy traffic lights.

Fitting a dynamo

1 The best modern dynamos do not leave you in the dark when you stop. They have a capacitor that charges up as you ride and this keeps the light going. They also have a voltage regulator to stop bulbs burning out going downhill.

2 Fit the dynamo mounting around the fork blade so that the roller lines up with the file pattern on the sidewall. Then loosen the angle bolt and adjust the position of the dynamo until the roller forms a right angle with the spokes.

High-visibility clothing

3 Check frequently that your lights are working at full power. If not, change the batteries. When replacing bulbs, do not touch the glass at all, especially if it is a halogen type. Keep spare bulbs and batteries at home.

1 Always dress in bright colors so that you get noticed when cycling, even during the day. But if you cycle a lot at night, go for a proper yellow cycling jersey with a reflective patch where it will show up best to motorists.

2 Foul weather clothing is available in many colors, but, fluorescent yellow is still the best. Some of the latest waterproof jackets also have flecks of reflective material. They shimmer in headlights and can not be ignored.

3 Cycling gloves padded with shock absorbent gel give you a more comfortable ride and protect hands from dirt and abrasions. But if you go for ones with a reflective back, they make your hand signals stand out at night.

CLEANING THE CONTACTS

All bike lights start to give problems eventually. To get them working properly again, remove the batteries and check the contacts for greenish deposits. Remove these with a screwdriver and spray with aerosol lube. Give the switch a squirt as well, turning it on and off several times so that the aerosol lube gets to all parts.

A FEW REFLECTIONS

Plastic reflective material is one of the best and cheapest road safety precautions there is. Compared with the tiny light output of almost any bike light, reflective materials are much more noticeable, throwing a bright and very noticeable patch of bright light back at other road users.

Among the best items are reflective arm and leg bands. These are almost always on the move, so they alert even the least alert driver to the fact that you are on the road and need room to maneuver. Safety belts that go around the shoulders and waist are not quite as effective You can also fix self-adhesive reflective material to frames, preferably to the back and the sides. However, pedal and wheel reflectors are probably the most effective items, although they will not fit on all pedals.

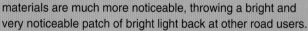

3 Remove the paint on the frame under the grub screw on the mounting clip, coat with petroleum jelly and refit. Earth the lights in the same way. Then run the wires to the front and rear lights, keeping them as short as possible.

4 To prevent wiring problems, attach all wires neatly to the frame with zip ties. Apply spray lube to the connections and tighten lightly with a wrench if necessary. Road test to check that the lights work properly.

Frame-fitted equipment

You can fit almost anything on a bike frame, from a tool kit to panniers with enough luggage space for a world tour.

For winter riding, fenders are more or less essential if you count on getting home from work or a ride fairly dry. Luckily, the quality of fenders and fender fittings has improved a lot in recent years. Even the thinnest aluminum fenders are now strong enough to support the weight of a bike.

Nevertheless, fenders always carry the danger of coming loose and getting caught in the wheel. If that happens, a nasty crash counts as coming off lightly, so tighten the frame and fender stay fixings frequently. Ideally, go for guards with a weak link that allows the stays to be ripped off the fender instead of catching in the wheel.

Luggage racks and carriers often share mounting points with fenders, although for enjoyable touring, separate mountings are a very big plus. Do not be tempted to compromise on the quality of racks or panniers because if they sway during cornering or threaten to burst open, they are a real misery.

You can also fit bags to the handlebars, but low-mounted front panniers on a proper rack are a better solution because they keep the center of gravity low, and that means better bike control.

On everyday bikes, a U-lock with a clip to mount it on the frame is the best security device. They are no problem to carry around, quality ones are available at reasonable prices, and they are always there when you want them. But you must always lock your bike to an immovable object and put the lock shackle around the wheel rim for full security.

Bottle bosses

1 Bottle cages are all designed to install standard bottle bosses. Just undo the screw in the boss—they usually have a socket head—position the cage, and replace the screw.

2 Full-size bike pumps are fitted to the frame. But mini-pumps can be mounted on clips that screw onto the bottle bosses under the bottle cage, making room for both.

Fitting fenders and racks

1 To install fenders to a sports or touring bike, remove the back brake and position the fender bridge roughly by eye. Then attach the seat stays to the fender eyelets loosely, slide the fender into place, and bolt the wire stays to the fender eyelets.

2 Slide the fender bridge so that the tab contacts the back of the brake bridge. Thread the brake fixing bolt through the tab and fit the nut and washer. Tighten up the tabs on the fender bridge with pliers, adjust the stay length, and tighten everything.

TASTELESS
Aluminum drinking bottles are expensive, but they are far less likely to add a nasty taste to your drink than plastic ones. In winter, well-equipped riders use vacuum flasks tailored to install the standard bottle cage.

Bicycle locks

1 Although heavy and ugly, the frame-mounted U-lock is one of the best ways of stopping thieves from going off with your bike. However, some riders prefer to save weight by using a lock and chain.

2 The lock holder is plastic-covered, so it will not damage your frame and only requires two screws to hold it there. Adjust the third screw so that when you fold the lever, the clip grips the lock securely.

3 When buying a U-lock, check that the shackle is large enough to go around a post, through your back wheel and frame and also through the front wheel rim, after taking it out of the forks.

LUBRICATE YOUR LOCK

Out in all weathers, bike locks need an occasional squirt of lubricant to keep the lock barrel turning sweetly. Give the holes that the U-shaped shackle fits into a squirt as well. Ideally, use a fairly thick chain lubricant containing Teflon so that there is a solid lubricant left on the lock parts, after the lube itself has been washed away in the rain. Keep a spare key at home.

3 If there are brazed-on eyelets fitted to the chainstays, bolt the top carrier mountings to them. Otherwise use the brake fixing bolt. Then bolt the rack supports to the frame via the fender eyelets. Use washers and self-locking nuts to prevent from it coming loose.

4 Once you have fitted a rack, you can carry some things using an elastic luggage strap. But do not let the strap dangle or it will get caught in the back wheel. Pannier bags allow you to carry much more. Ideally, they should be tailored to fit the rack you are using.

5 If you do not want to install normal fenders, there is a large range of clip-on guards that will do the job well. Some just clamp onto the down tube and hang in mid-air, others are specially designed for MTBs with cantis or V brakes, and others fit sports bikes.

CATCH CRUD

Crud catchers take only a few moments to install onto the down tube of a normal style MTB. They are held in place either by strong elastic straps or with touch-and-close fastenings, so they can be fitted in moments if rain seems to threaten.

Crud catchers can be fitted to frames of almost any shape, including Y-frames. However, they can only cope with light rain and mud, not a deluge.

Seats for kids

Occasionally ideas from the auto industry cross over into the world of bikes. This child safety seat is one of the best so far.

Nearly all child seats are made from molded plastic. The designs are strongly influenced by the child seats used in cars and the net result is that it is now quite practical to think of carrying kids weighing up to about 40 pounds to the play group or the shops.

Different makers of child seats offer different features. The type shown here can be fitted without interfering with an existing luggage carrier and, once the basic fittings are in place, it is a matter of seconds to install the seat and remove it. This type also has foot rests that rule out any possibility of small feet getting caught in the wheel, soft cushioning, and an effective shoulder harness. The design of the stay and the clamps ensures it can be fitted to almost any bike, although there are plenty of other good designs that are fitted in roughly the same way.

Other types fit on a luggage carrier using a simple slide-on mounting. Unfortunately, this rules out carrying any luggage at all, but most riders find a child is enough of a handicap anyway. On the other hand, if there are several bikes in the family, the seat can be swapped between them simply by fitting them all with the correct type of carrier.

1 Fit the main frame clamp onto the down tube and test-fit the seat so you can raise or lower it to the correct height. Tighten the fixing bolts, but not hard. Test-fit the seat to check the height for the seat stay supports next. When you have got them about right, tighten up the fixings. Then check that the seat fits easily onto the lugs and that the stay fits into the main frame clamp.

2 Adjust the position of the clamps and supports, if necessary, to ensure the front end of the stay fits easily into the clamp. Then press the red plastic locking tab down to hold it firmly in place.

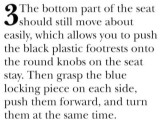

3 The bottom part of the seat should still move about easily, which allows you to push the black plastic footrests onto the round knobs on the seat stay. Then grasp the blue locking piece on each side, push them forward, and turn them at the same time.

ADJUSTABLE BACKREST

The backrest of this seat can be adjusted with the large knob at the front. So if the child is sleeping, the backrest can be wound down and he or she can be placed in the seat without waking. Extra clamps can be obtained so the seat can be moved from bike to bike.

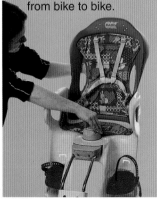

4 Turn the locking pieces through 90° to lock the seat in place. The seat should now be positioned well above the back wheel and the luggage carrier, and should feel firm and stable. The seat should be as close to the saddle as possible to prevent it from swaying.

5 The carrier is now ready to use. Check that your child's feet are in the rests and adjust the harness to prevent squirming. To remove the seat, just lift the red locking tab and turn the blue locking pieces, then pull the seat back and off.

Bikes on cars

The best way for city dwellers to enjoy the countryside is to ship the bikes out by car, leaving the crowded urban areas far behind.

Roof racks are probably the best way of transporting bikes. On the positive side, there is enough room for up to four machines, the bikes do not get covered in road dust, and you can get to the luggage area without difficulty. On the other hand, they are not easy to load and create noise as well as aerodynamic drag. Rail-type bike carriers, which hold a bike upright on both wheels, can be fitted to nearly all roof racks. The bike is usually supported by an arm and this sometimes locks in place to improve theft resistance. The alternative way of fitting a bike to a roof rack uses a standard wheel quick-release fitted to the front of the roof rack. The forks are slotted in, without the front wheel, which reduces the aerodynamic effects and improves the car's steering in crosswinds.

Trunk-, tailgate-, and tow-bar-mounted bike carriers create less noise and less aerodynamic drag, but when loaded, the back lights and license plate are nearly always obscured. This is, of course, illegal. The only way around this is to wire the car for a light board and strap it on the stack of bikes every time.

Tow-bar-mounted racks are more secure than the strap-on type and come in two varieties. One type has a pair of horizontal arms and you simply throw the bikes on. The other type has tubular wheel supports and is still more secure. You can even obtain racks specially designed for off-road vehicles with the spare wheel mounted at the back.

Tow bar mounting

Tow bar-mounted bike carriers are probably the best of all designs, though they also tend to be the most expensive. A mounting plate is bolted semi-permanently behind the tow ball, into which the pole of the carrier is slotted. In this deluxe type, up to three bikes can be slotted into place, a strap is then passed around them and tightened with a ratchet. This holds the bikes very firmly, but the trunk can still be opened all the way. The light board is the only serious drawback.

Roof rack mounting

This car has a standard roof rack bolted to the gutters and fitted with rail carriers. But if your car is fitted with roof rails, you can usually fit custom-made cross bars supplied by the main dealer or speciality accessory suppliers. On the other hand, modern cars without gutters need special roof rack mountings.

Strap-on bike carrier

Two bikes or more can be squeezed onto a strap-on trunk rack. These work fine on hatchbacks, where you can get to the luggage from inside the car, but not so well on sedans. The big drawback is that on older designs, the bikes cover up the license plate. Only the latest high-level carriers avoid this problem.

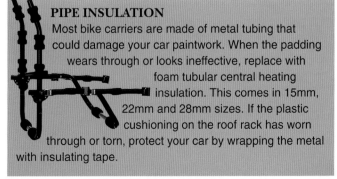

PIPE INSULATION
Most bike carriers are made of metal tubing that could damage your car paintwork. When the padding wears through or looks ineffective, replace with foam tubular central heating insulation. This comes in 15mm, 22mm and 28mm sizes. If the plastic cushioning on the roof rack has worn through or torn, protect your car by wrapping the metal with insulating tape.

WHAT DOES THAT MEAN?

This section explains the meaning of words commonly used by bike enthusiasts, including words that have entered biking 'language' since the advent of mountain bikes.

A

AHEADSET: *Japanese/American brand of headset. Can only be used with specially designed forks and stem. Most manufacturers now make a similar set up.*

ALLEN KEY: *Six-sided, l-shaped bar of metal that fits into the socket of a socket head bolt. Available individually, in sets, and on a ring. Referred to as a hex key here.*

ALLOY: *Usually short for aluminum alloy. A mixture of metals which is usually better than a pure one.*

ALLOY RIMS: *All decent quality bikes have wheel rims made of aluminum alloy. Steel is the alternative material but the braking surface is so smooth that it is hard to stop quickly, even with pads specially formulated for use with this material.*

ANTI-SEIZE GREASE: *Alight grease containing powdered metal, usually copper. The grease eventually evaporates, leaving the copper behind, which acts as a lubricant.*

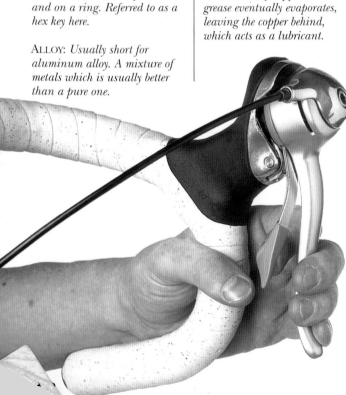

AXLE: *The central part of a bearing assembly.*

B

BALL BEARING: *Usually means a hard-chromed, perfectly round, steel ball that fits between the cup and cone in bike bearings. Also means the complete assembly of inner and outer race plus ball bearings, as used in a cartridge bottom bracket.*

BAR ENDS: *Look like cow horns bolted to the ends of straight handlebars. They give an alternative hand position, especially useful for hill climbing or in traffic.*

BEADS: *The stiff edge of a tire. Usually made of wire but occasionally of Kevlar.*

BEARINGS: *Any part designed to minimize the wear in a rotating or sliding assembly. On a bike the main bearings are the headset, bottom bracket, and hub bearings.*

BOTTLE BOSS: *Threaded frame fitting used for attaching bottle cages to the frame.*

BOTTOM BRACKET: *The bearings and axle that carry the crankset.*

BOTTOM BRACKET SHELL: *The housing at the bottom of the seat and down tubes into which the bottom bracket is fitted.*

BRAKE MODULATOR: *Adjusts the amount of force needed to apply the brake.*

BRAZED-ON FITTING: *Items like bottle bosses and lever bosses fixed to the frame.*

BUTT: *The thickened end of a tube. See double butted.*

C

CABLE END CAP: *A soft metal sleeve that can be crimped onto the end of a cable to prevent it fraying.*

CABLE STOP: *A hollow tube brazed on to the frame. The outer cable fits into the open end, while the inner cable passes out of the other. Often slotted so that you can pull the outer cable out, without disconnecting the inner one—useful when lubricating the inner cable.*

CANTILEVER BRAKES: *Attached to the frame via pivots on the fork blades and chain stays. Powerful brakes, fitted to most mountain bikes because mud*

does not build up around them. Also used on hybrids and touring bikes.

CARBON FIBER: *High-strength, high-cost material used for making frames, seat posts ,and other components.*

CARTRIDGE BOTTOM BRACKET: *Bottom bracket bearing in which the axle runs on standard ball bearings, sealed inside a metal sleeve.*

CASSETTE: *A set of 7, 8, 9 or 10 sprockets which mount onto a freehub body. The freewheel mechanism fits between the freehub body and the freewheel itself.*

CENTER PULL BRAKES: *A brake with two separate arms independently mounted on a back plate. Powerful and reliable but no longer made.*

CENTER TO CENTER: *Usual way of measuring frame size. Distance from center of bracket axle to center of top tube. The measurement can be given in either inches or centimeters – it makes no difference.*

CENTERING: *Usually refers to adjusting the position of a brake in such a way that the brake pads are equally spaced from the braking surface. Can also refer to installing a back wheel so that it is equally spaced between the chain stays.*

CHAIN GUARD: *Usually a light steel device that wraps around the chain, protecting the rider. Fixed to the frame with clips.*

CHAIN STAY: *The tube that runs between the bottom bracket and the drop out. It is usually oval near the bottom bracket.*

CHAINRING: *The toothed part of the crankset which engages with the chain. Often removable.*

CRANKSET: *The chainrings, spider, and cranks are known collectively as the crankset.*

CHROME MOLYBDENUM OR CHROMOLY: *A steel alloy often used for bike frames. Though not a high-quality material, chrome molybdenum steel is ideal for budget-priced bikes.*

CLINCHERS: *Detachable tires that are held onto the wheel rim by stiff beads that clinch under the open edges of the rim.*

CLUSTER: *Usually short for sprocket cluster.*

COGS: *People often speak of the chainring and sprockets as cogs because they are toothed. Not a correct use of the word.*

COLUMBUS: *Italian maker of high-quality frame tubing.*

COTTERLESS CRANKS: *Cranks that bolt onto the end of the bottom bracket axle.*

COTTER PINS: *Tapered steel pins with one flat side that hold the cranks onto the bottom bracket axle. Seldom found on recent bikes.*

CRANKS: *Metal components that carry the pedals and transmit rider's energy to the chainring.*

CUP AND CONE BEARING: *The standard bike bearing assembly consisting of ball bearings trapped between the semi-circular cup and the tapered cone. These bearings are adjusted by moving the screwed part in or out until they turn freely, without any play.*

D

DEGREASER: *Any solvent that will dissolve grease. Includes paraffin, diesel fuel, and various specially formulated, ecologically acceptable brand-name products.*

DERAILLEUR: *French word for gearing systems that work by 'derailing' the chain from one sprocket to another.*

DERAILLEUR HANGER: *The piece of metal that attaches the rear derailleur to the frame. Can be separate from, or part of, the frame.*

DIAMOND FRAME: *The standard shape for a bike frame. Mountain bikes usually have a modified diamond frame.*

DISC BRAKE: *A brake that uses a rotor fitted to the hub and a caliper mounted on the fork leg or chain stay.*

DOUBLE BUTTED: *Used to describe frame tubing which is drawn thin in the middle for lightness and thicker at the ends where maximum strength is needed.*

DOWN TUBE: *Usually the largest diameter part of the frame. Runs from the head tube to the bottom bracket.*

DROP OUT: *Part of the frame that carries the front or back wheel.*

DUAL PIVOT BRAKES: *A cross between side pull and center pull brakes. More compact than center pulls and more powerful than side pulls.*

E

EXPANDER BOLT: *Long bolt that fits into the upright part of the stem and screws into the cone or wedge that locks the stem into the frame.*

F

FIXED GEAR: *A single sprocket screwed on to the rear hub, without a freewheel. All the time that the bike is moving, the rider has to pedal.*

FORK CROWN: *The top part of the forks. Sometimes it is separate, sometimes it is formed out of the fork blade itself.*

FORK END: *The part of the fork that carries the front wheel.*

FORKS: *The steerable part of the frame that holds the front wheel.*

FRAME ANGLES: *The angle between the top tube and seat tube, and between the top tube and head tube. Greatly influences how the frame behaves on the road.*

FREEHUB: *A very popular design of rear hub which has the sprocket cluster built in.*

Suitable for 7-, 8-, 9-, and 10-speed set-ups, the right hand hub bearing fits inside the freewheel mechanism.

FREEWHEEL: *Nearly all sprockets are mounted on a freewheel mechanism which allows you to coast along without pedaling.*

FRONT DERAILLEUR: *Swaps the chain from one chainring to another. Two chainrings multiplies the number of gears by two. Three chainrings multiplies the number by three.*

G

GEAR RANGE: *The gap between the lowest gear and the highest.*

GEAR RATIO: *On bikes, this is the amount that the bike will move for each revolution of the*

cranks. On a low gear, this is about 1 m (40 in) per revolution and around 2.7 m (110 in) on a high one.

H

HAMMER: *A tool that should only be used with caution.*

HEADSET: *The top and bottom bearings that support the forks and allow them to turn, thus providing steering. The bottom bearing is subject to very heavy loads and must be replaced when dents form in the bearing track.*

HEAD TUBE: *The shortest frame tube. Fits between the top and down tubes. Can be so short as to be almost non-existent on very small frames.*

HIGH GEAR: *A gear ratio in which you travel a long way for every revolution of the cranks. In high, the chain is on the largest chainring and one of the smallest sprockets.*

HUB GEARS: *The alternative system to derailleur gears. Contained within an enlarged rear hub. 3-, 5- and 7-speed versions are now available but they all tend to be heavy and absorb a lot of energy.*

HYBRID: *Type of bike combining some mountain bike components and frame features with large wheels and a fairly normal design of frame.*

I

INDEXED GEARS: *Derailleur gears with a shifter that has click stops indicating each gear position.*

J

JOCKEY WHEELS: *Small wheels that guide the chain around the sprockets and towards the chainring.*

K

KEVLAR: *High-strength artificial fiber used for reinforcing tires and other components.*

KNOBBIES: *Deeply treaded tires designed for high grip in mud.*

L

LOW GEAR: *A gear ratio in which you move a short distance for every revolution of the cranks. Used for climbing hills and off-road.*

LUBE: *Short for lubricant.*

LUG: *A complex steel sleeve used to join the main tubes of a frame.*

N

NIPPLE: *The metal nut that passes through the rim and screws on to the spoke. Spokes are tensioned by tightening up the nipple.*

P

PHILLIPS SCREWDRIVER: *Screwdriver with cross-shaped tip. Sizes 1 and 2 are both used on bikes and are not interchangeable.*

PLAY: *Unwanted movement in a bearing. Can be due to wear or improper adjustment. Sometimes spoken of as 'a couple of millimeters play' or similar.*

PRESTA VALVE: *Found mainly on racing bike tires. Has a*

knurled section on the end to keep it closed.

Q

QUICK RELEASE: *Usually refers to the mechanism that allows you to remove a bike wheel with just a turn of the quick release lever. Can also refer to other quick release (q/r) components like seat post clamps and panniers.*

R

RACE: *Part of a bearing assembly in contact with the ball bearings.*

REAR DERAILLEUR: *The rear gear mechanism that moves the chain up and down the rear sprocket. Deals with up to 10 sprockets.*

REYNOLDS: *British makers of high-quality steel tubing for frames.*

RIM: *The part of the wheel on which the tire is mounted.*

S

SCHRADER VALVE: *The car-type tire valve that has a separate insert. Larger in diameter than a Presta valve.*

SEAT POST: *Tube that fits into the seat tube and supports the saddle.*

SEAT STAY: *The small-diameter tube that runs between the seat lug and the drop out.*

SEAT TUBE: *The large-diameter frame tube which supports the saddle.*

SHIFTER: *Refers to any mechanism for changing gear.*

SIDE PULL BRAKE: *Type of brake used on road bikes. Both brake arms are connected to the brake cable on one side of the unit.*

SIDEWALL: *The area of a tire between the tread and the wheel rim. Often a yellow color that contrasts with the black of the tread.*

SLICKS: *Smooth tires used on mountain bikes for road riding.*

SPOKE: *The thin wire component that connects the hub to the rim.*

SPRINTS: *A very light combination of wheels and tires used solely for road and track racing. The tube is sewn into the tire and the whole thing is then stuck to the rim.*

SPRAY LUBE: *Refers to various brands of silicon-based aerosol lubricant. Also to the specialist bike-type, which contains a solid lubricant that remains after the liquid part has evaporated.*

SPROCKET: *The toothed wheel or wheels attached to the back wheel that transfer drive from the chain to the hub.*

SPROCKET CLUSTER: *Collective name for all the sprockets of a derailleur gear system.*

STEERER TUBE: *The tube that fits into the fork crown and is supported by the headset. Turns with the fork.*

STEM: *Fits into the steerer tube and supports the handlebars.*

STI: *A gear-changing system made by Shimano in which the shifters are built in to the brake levers.*

STRADDLE CABLE: *Short cable that joins two independent brake arms. Found on some cantilever and all center pull brakes.*

SUSPENSION FORKS: *Forks that allow the front wheel to move up and down to absorb bumps. The movement is usually controlled by some sort of spring and a gas or fluid damper mechanism.*

T

TOE-IN: *Usually measured in millimeters. Refers to fitting brake pads closer to the rim at the front than at the back.*

TOP TUBE: *The tube joining the seat tube to the head tube. It is usually horizontal but increasing numbers of bikes have a sloping top tube.*

TRANSMISSION: *All the components that deal with transmitting power from the rider's legs to the back wheel. That means crankset, chain and sprockets, plus the front and rear derailleurs.*

TUBULARS: *A tire where the tube is sewn into the tread part. Used mostly by road racers.*

TIRE VALVE: *Device that holds air pressure in a center. On a bike, the valve is actually part of the tube.*

TIRE – 700C: *The type of tire normally fitted to good-quality road bikes with 27in wheels. Thin, light, and strong.*

V

'V' BRAKE: *A new design of cantilever brake. The brake arms fit standard pivot bosses but are vertical, which increases leverage and allows the cable to pull directly on the brake arm.*

W

WHEEL RIM: *The outer part of a bike wheel that carries the tire. Also the braking surfaces. Can be made of steel or alloy.*

WISHBONE STAY: *A design of chainstay in which the two tubes join above the back wheel and are connected to the seat cluster by a larger single tube.*

park pro cable cutter
$31

INDEX

THE AUTHOR AND PUBLISHER WOULD LIKE TO THANK

◆ Alan Hewitt and Peter Harrison of Shimano (Madison Cycles)
◆ Graham Snodden of SRAM
◆ Fu Wong of Peugeot
◆ Peter Plummer of Venhill Engineering
◆ Phil Rickaby and David Jack of Raleigh Parts and Accessories
◆ Wayne Shepherd and Chris Carter of Halfords
◆ James Tatlow and Duncan Cruxton of Zoo-Bits (RST)
◆ George Longhurst of George Longhurst Cycles
◆ Mike Dyason
◆ Jason Boness of E. Reece
◆ Douglas Gill International
◆ Michelin Tires
◆ Marco Oldrati of Campagnolo
◆ Madison Cycles
◆ Bob Elliot for FAG
◆ Freestyle Sports
◆ Selle Bassano
◆ Caratti Sport
◆ Zyro
◆ John Edwards of Moore Large
◆ Continental Tires
◆ Yeovil Cycle Center

◆ From the author, particular thanks to Jeremy Phillips, who made an enormous contribution to every aspect of this book. Also to Tim Ridley, whose photographic work is outstanding
◆ Rob Parker, Jason Youé and Bernie Goldrick for all their efforts in getting the pictures and words right
◆ Paul Buckland and Peter Trott of the Haynes Project Workshop
◆ Jill Gough and Judy Bailey

Photographic credits
Key: t top, b bottom, l left, r right, m middle
Nick Pope: 36bl, bm, br; 37
Stockfile:4bl, br; 5; 17
Front Cover: Image Bank (Kenneth Redding); Tim Ridley, Steve Behr and Stockfile (Steve Behr, Bob Smith, Mark Gallup and Sue Darlow)
For the third edition: SRAM, Venhill Engineering, E.Reece/Univega, Dawes Cycles